The Psychotherapy
Documentation Primer

The Psychotherapy Documentation Primer

DONALD E. WIGER

JOHN WILEY & SONS, INC.

New York • Chichester • Weinheim • Brisbane • Singapore • Toronto

Diagnostic criteria taken from DSM-IV reprinted with permission from
the Diagnostic and Statistical Manual of Mental Disorders, Fourth Edition.
Copyright 1994 American Psychiatric Association.

This book is printed on acid-free paper. ∞

This publication is designed to provide accurate and authoritative information in regard to the subject matter covered. It is sold with the understanding that the publisher is not engaged in rendering professional services. If legal, accounting, medical, psychological or any other expert assistance is required, the services of a competent professional person should be sought.

Library of Congress Cataloging-in-Publication Data:

Wiger, Donald E., 1953–
      The psychotherapy documentation primer / Donald E. Wiger.
            p.   cm.
      Includes index.
      ISBN 0-471-28990-6 (pbk. : alk. paper)
      1. Psychiatry—Medical records—Forms.   2. Mental health services—
      Medical records—Forms.   3. Mental health services—Management.
      4. Medical economics.   I. Title.
      RC455.2.M38W543   1999
      616.89'14'068—dc21   98-18229

Printed in the United States of America.

10   9   8   7   6   5   4   3

This book is dedicated to Helen Lockery of Maplewood, MN.

Mom, I want to thank you for being there consistently all of my life. You have been a blessing to so many people. Perhaps no one has ever thanked you for the sacrifice you chose to make by leaving high school early to help support your family. Now, I will always be there for you. I don't exactly know what it is about you (there are many great things), but you did a great job in raising a son who is a state senator, a daughter who is a hard-working, giving, and warm person, and me. We have all done very well in life because of your example. You taught each of us to make a difference in other people's lives.

Practice Planner Series Preface

The practice of psychotherapy has a dimension that did not exist 30, 20, or even 15 years ago—accountability. Treatment programs, public agencies, clinics, and even group and solo practitioners must now justify the treatment of patients to outside review entities that control the payment of fees. This development has resulted in an explosion of paperwork.

Clinicians must now document what has been done in treatment, what is planned for the future, and what the anticipated outcomes of the interventions are. The books and software in this Practice Planner series are designed to help practitioners fulfill these documentation requirements efficiently and professionally.

The Practice Planner series is growing rapidly. It now includes not only the original *Complete Psychotherapy Treatment Planner* and the *Child and Adolescent Psychotherapy Treatment Planner,* but also *Treatment Planners* targeted to specialty areas of practice, including: chemical dependency, the continuum of care, couples therapy, older adult treatment, employee assistance, pastoral counseling, and more.

In addition to the *Treatment Planners,* the series also includes *TheraScribe®: The Computerized Assistant to Psychotherapy Treatment Planning* and *TheraBiller™: The Computerized Mental Health Office Manager,* as well as adjunctive books, such as the *Brief Therapy, Chemical Dependence, Couples,* and *Child Homework Planners, The Psychotherapy Documentation Primer,* and *Clinical, Forensic, Child, Couples and Family,* and *Chemical Dependence Documentation Sourcebooks*—containing forms and resources to aid in mental health practice management. The goal of the series is to provide practitioners with the resources they need in order to provide high-quality care in the era of accountability—or, to put it simply, we seek to help you spend more time on patients, and less on paperwork.

Arthur E. Jongsma, Jr.
Grand Rapids, Michigan
Series Editor

Preface

My career began as a minister. Documentation for this profession was rudimentary; its unique managed care guidelines hadn't changed for nearly 2000 years, and there were no insurance forms to submit. Treatment plans were eternal and case notes nonexistent. Although I enjoyed working with people, the cloth wasn't for me. In the early 1980s, I returned to college for graduate work in psychology. After earning a doctorate, I worked in a few positions gaining experience as a psychologist.

In early 1991, I founded a mental health clinic in Blaine, Minnesota. Since the office space had been vacant for over a year, the landlord agreed to let me have the first two months' rent free if I signed a lease. The office furniture consisted of my family's living room furniture and all the pictures we had hanging in our apartment. Beyond expectations, the clinic grew rapidly. Within a few months, two employees were working full-time and more were needed. The clinic was soon financially sound, providing a variety of services, and developing a solid reputation in the community. We learned the marketing secrets to obtaining referrals and managed care contracts. More clinics were opened. My family and I were able to move from an apartment to a comfortable house. We drove new cars. Our fourth and fifth children were born. It felt like success—the American dream.

Then in 1993 I received a phone call from an insurance auditor. She stated that we were being audited because it was unusual for a new clinic to conduct so much business after only two years. My academic training and professional experience in no way prepared me for such an event. For the next few days, auditors searched through and copied dozens of charts and asked seemingly hundreds of questions that made little sense to me at the time. Every audited client chart contained an intake, assessment report, treatment plan, and progress notes for each session. I thought the auditors would be impressed. Imagine my surprise when phrases such as "no evidence of medical necessity," "lack of clear documentation," and "progress notes do not match treatment objectives," filled the office, over, and over, and over.

No sooner had I begun thanking the auditors for the education they had provided me and telling them how I would change my written ways than they asked me how I would like to make the payback. At this point, I no longer felt successful; rather, I began scrimping for the thousands of dollars that had to be returned to the insurance company due to poor documentation.

At the debriefing, the auditors told me I had done nothing wrong therapeutically or ethically, but that the charts were poorly written or "not in compliance," as they put it. Even though our clients had needed and benefited from our services, the documentation did not provide adequate evidence of treatment outcomes. I learned the hard way that, "If it isn't written down, it doesn't exist."

Today, much has changed since that audit. Last year I phoned my auditors and thanked them again for the education their audit had provided. That audit changed my view regarding the clinician's accountability in therapy. In addition to the financial necessity for thorough documentation, I learned that, ethically, clinicians have a responsibility to clearly document what is taking place in therapy. Accurate documentation communicates the course of therapy and provides the necessary information to determine its effectiveness. Accurate documentation also keeps therapy on target. Ultimately, the client benefits the most.

Before the audit, I had never learned how to prepare proper case documentation, nor did I know it was an issue. Since then, I have learned how to properly document charts. In the process, I was surprised at how few books existed on the topic. In fact, much of the current literature in documentation procedures comes from the nursing and education professions.

Since the audit, I have taught documentation skills seminars to several thousand mental health professionals. Many therapists have related stories similar to my audit encounter. Each time they have told me, "I was never taught how to document."

Now that I've learned the methods of proper documentation, I have not paid back a cent to third-party payors. The more I learn about documentation, psychopathology, and effective treatment principles, the less time it takes to conduct intakes and write treatment plans and progress notes. It made more sense to me to write a book than travel around the country telling people what I've learned.

The Psychotherapy Documentation Primer guides the therapist through the entire documentation process, providing clinical examples that meet regulatory agency and third-party requirements. The book also helps the clinician learn to appreciate the positive effects of clinical documentation. These include but are not limited to:

1. Spending less time in paperwork procedures.

2. Decreasing uncertainty as to what to document.

3. Increasing compliance with third-party requirements and ensuring audit survival.

4. Helping the client by documenting the need for initial and additional services.

5. Learning means of keeping therapy on target through effective documentation.

6. Heightening communication with other professionals.

7. Documenting a specific course of therapy.

8. Demonstrating the effects and outcomes of therapeutic procedures.

This text is designed to be used in conjunction with each of the Treatment Planners in the Wiley series. *The Complete Psychotherapy Treatment Primer* provides specific treatment plan examples of problem areas, goals, objectives, and treatment strategies written to meet third-party and regulatory agency requirements. It is designed to follow *DSM-IV* criteria for addressing mental health disorders and follows currently accepted treatment strategies; thus, it is an invaluable time-saving tool.

DONALD E. WIGER

Acknowledgments

Special thanks are due to two extraordinary people who have helped me in editorial matters and ideas. Tracey Thornblade provided excellent editorial advice and posed questions that increased the quality and flow of information in this work. Kelly Franklin, Executive Editor and Associate Publisher at John Wiley & Sons, has guided me through the publication process for two books. She helped me stay on schedule and provided much encouragement and professional advice during the writing process. This teamwork approach has made the entire authoring experience a pleasure.

Contents

The Psychotherapy
Documentation Primer

1

Introduction

In this age of clinical accountability, *The Psychotherapy Documentation Primer* is intended to teach mental health clinicians and graduate students clinical documentation procedures that meet current criteria established by third-party payors and regulating agencies such as the Joint Commission of Accreditation of Healthcare Organizations (JCAHO). Accurate documentation that communicates the entire scope of therapy is crucial to financial and professional survival. Regulatory agencies and third-party payors unequivocally require that each step of the clinical process be clearly documented to preserve clinical integrity and accountability within the profession. Third-party payors impose strict guidelines to help contain costs and only pay for services clearly documented to be medically necessary.

Although there are several reasons to learn good documentation procedures, the main benefit is ethics. The therapist is accountable for the services rendered in all phases of the therapy process. Without good documentation, there is no clear record of the course and progress of therapy. Sloppy clinical procedures are not only unfair to the client, but they may border on malpractice. Billing for unnecessary or unhelpful services creates an ethical concern. Without adequate documentation, only the clinician and client know what took place in the session. When sound documentation procedures are followed, a written record of treatment will be available to third parties. Responsible clinicians will continue to provide clients with valuable services, whereas those who are prone to cutting corners will now be required to provide evidence of the effectiveness of their services.

Utilizing proper documentation methods also reduces the threat of financial ruin resulting from large audit penalties.

Therapists want to help their clients, but to do so they must stay in business. Sound documentation bridges the gap.

Third-party payors no longer blindly accept billing for any psychotherapy services. They require specific types of evidence demonstrating the need and benefits of treatment and require therapy to be conducted in a time-efficient manner. Without knowing proper documentation procedures and how to present a case on paper, the therapist is vulnerable to appearing to be "out of compliance" or appearing to provide "unnecessary services."

The vast majority of mental health therapists provide invaluable services to their clients but have little or no training in how to document the evidence of their skills. After learning and employing proper documentation techniques, most therapists report feeling much more at ease and confident about meeting third-party requirements. They become more aware of therapeutic progress.

Third-party payors will reimburse therapists from all treatment modalities (e.g., cognitive, behavioral, dynamic, solution-focused) provided they have demonstrated clinical effectiveness in treatment (i.e., by consistently documenting alleviation of client mental health impairments in a reasonable time period). Therapeutic modalities from client insight, to cognitive-behavior theory, to existentialism are divergent, but each has its own therapeutic merits. As a result, variation in therapeutic techniques is both expected and encouraged. Managed care companies, along with other third-party payors, are open to this variation, provided that improvements in client functioning are documented. However, not much variation is allowed in documenting the effect of services. Regulatory agencies require that the same measuring stick be used to assess the effects of therapy regardless of the treatment modality employed. The current measurement standards in mental health require that clinical documentation be observable, measurable, and provide behavioral evidence of therapeutic progress. Clinical opinions that lack proper documentation to support them are considered inadequate by today's standards.

Behavioral evidence for documentation does not mean that treatment must be from a behavioral school of thought. Rather, therapeutic effects must be demonstrated in behavioral terms. That is, "What changes in behavior are taking place as a result of therapy?"

The course of clinical documentation begins with the initial intake. Intake data provides information for preparing the treatment plan. All information in the treatment plan must be documented. However, the treatment plan should not include problem areas not clearly validated during assessment. Progress notes are based on the treatment plan. The bulk of the progress notes should reflect the diagnosis and treatment plan objectives. Documentation materials, such as the initial assessment, treatment plan, and progress notes, are thus interrelated rather than separate entities.

Most of the documentation examples offered in this text represent a client with depression. Appendix A presents the documented chart of a client diagnosed with Panic Disorder with Agoraphobia. This case, which is documented from initial intake to termination of treatment, represents the type of information that should be available to a third-party reviewer.

Before considering each step of the therapeutic process and the correspondent documentation that should be made, it is necessary to understand what constitutes proper documentation. In addition, it is important to know what kind of documentation third-party payors require and how the course of therapy should be charted.

HIGHLIGHTS
of Chapter 1

★ Accurate and specific documentation procedures are necessary for ethical, professional, legal, and financial reasons.

★ Third-party payors are becoming much more stringent in procedures of accountability.

★ The intake, treatment plan, and progress notes are integrated items, each affecting and dependent upon each other. Although they are independent documents, they represent a continuous process in therapy.

★ Each step in the counseling procedures has specific documentation procedures which, if not followed, could be detrimental to both the client and therapist.

★ When accurate documentation procedures are incorporated, both the therapist and client benefit.

2

Overview of Current Documentation Procedures and Third-Party Requirements

Until the 1980s, mental health clinical documentation procedures consisted of little more than verifying that an interview took place, noting a diagnosis, and writing progress notes. Other than clinical judgment, few requirements were necessary to validate the diagnosis. Progress notes merely confirmed that a session took place. Third-party payors accepted on faith the validity of the diagnosis, need for services, and subsequent treatment procedures. Few clients questioned their diagnosis or were even aware that a diagnosis was given. Times have changed!

In this age of accountability, clinical skills are not measured solely by the therapist's ability to effect constructive changes in the client's life. Without adequate documentation, the best course of therapy appears ineffective on paper. Proper documentation also justifies the provision or continuation of treatment. A case manager relies on such paperwork to validate the effectiveness of treatment. The adage, "If it isn't written down, it doesn't exist," holds especially true for clinical documentation. Today, no assumptions are made regarding the need for services, what took place in a session, or what progress has occurred. Auditors or reviewers cannot attend therapy sessions to assess progress. The only effective means of communication therapists have with auditors is *documentation*. This book provides examples and explanations of how to document the entire course of psychotherapy.

WHAT WE "OUGHT TO DO" VERSUS WHAT WE WERE "TAUGHT TO DO"

Third-party payment for mental health services is generally based on a medical model of understanding and documenting client problems. Graduate training programs in psychotherapy vary tremendously in their clinical emphasis, ranging from focusing on personal growth to treating severe psychopathology. Clinicians whose training emphasizes the former are likely to be less comfortable with the medical model based on criteria found in the *Diagnostic and Statistical Manual of Mental Disorders, Fourth Edition* (American Psychiatric Association, 1994) than those whose training encompasses more chronic mental health concerns and specific Axis I and Axis II issues. The danger is that clinicians whose training does not include a pathology model may conduct and document counseling or psychotherapy in a manner that is therapeutically beneficial but may not be reimbursable by current third-party standards. Documentation training will help ease the discrepancy.

MENTAL HEALTH TRAINING

Current training in mental health programs tends to focus on quality of treatment and provides little emphasis on quality of documentation. Textbooks used in graduate training aptly present a variety of perspectives regarding assessment, diagnosis, theory, therapeutic practice, ethics, statistics, research design, and other professional areas. Most texts on treatment planning teach students how to plan treatment but not how to write and follow through with a treatment plan. Likewise, excellent books about how to conduct therapy exist, but they rarely teach students how to document what took place as a result of therapy.

Graduate school administrators often state that students will learn how to document the course of therapy during their practicum and internship experiences. This is generally not the case, however, because the clients seen in practicum and internship situations are usually treated pro bono or for a low cash fee. Thus, because third-party payment rarely covers services conducted by students, students' documentation is not subject to traditional third-party regulations. Clinical supervision tends to focus on the quality of therapy and case conceptualization—skills which, in themselves, are an arduous task to master. For these reasons, students' documentation skills are not typically scrutinized with the same rigor by their clinical supervisors as they would be by a third-party payor. Nevertheless, an increasing number of students are learning documentation skills after reporting this deficit in their training.

Third-Party Payors

The trend toward mental health counseling reimbursement by third-party payors is relatively new. Lobbying on the part of mental health professionals and employers has led, over the past few decades, to the inclusion of provisions for mental health care in standard insurance coverage. Over the past 10 years, however, mental health provisions have been increasingly restricted. There was a time in which, if a client's insurance policy covered mental health services, he or she could receive seemingly unlimited services from his or her choice of providers. Mental health professionals simply filled out the insurance forms and soon received payment. Not surprisingly, some people with minor diagnoses spent several years in counseling. As a result, the cost of mental health benefits skyrocketed, and insurance companies had to find means to lower costs to remain competitive. Managed care has flourished in this atmosphere.

Managed care changed the scope and nature of mental health services. Prior to managed care, it was possible to receive mental health counseling for issues like personal growth because mental health benefits were loosely defined in insurance policies. Therapists or clinicians trained in medical and nonmedical models alike prospered in the field. As managed care began providing coverage at lower rates, costs had to be lowered by limiting mental health benefits. The medical model offered an effective means of achieving those needs.

Clear and thorough documentation enables therapists from all schools of thought and insurers to track therapeutic progress. Without good documentation, there is no means to gauge the effects of treatment. Although practitioners from different treatment modalities disagree about which therapeutic methods lead to effective client change, documentation is neutral. Good documentation skills enable any therapist from any school of thought to demonstrate the need for services and demonstrate therapeutic effectiveness.

MEDICAL NECESSITY

The medical model, which requires "medical necessity" to qualify for third-party payment, has influenced current third-party reimbursement procedures for mental health services. In this case, medical necessity is defined as the need for professional services due to the existence of a mental disorder that has resulted in significant functional impairments. Prior to adopting the medical necessity model, third-party payors paid for services whenever qualified clinicians diagnosed clients with a mental health disorder. But the mere endorsement of symptoms of a *DSM-IV* diagnosis, without evidence of functional impairments or dysfunction, is no longer sufficient to warrant a diagnosis (or reimbursement for treatment).

Even people without diagnosable psychopathology exhibit at least trace characteristics of many *DSM-IV* diagnoses during their lifetime. For example, most people at times feel dysphoric, desire to be alone, experience anxiety, have creative thoughts, become suspicious of others, think about what would happen if they were dead, have issues with authority, and so on. Usually, the transient onset of trace or mild symptoms indicates normal life stressors rather than psychopathology. The degree to which symptoms affect the client's behavior and functioning is much more significant than acknowledging that symptoms exist. To qualify for treatment reimbursement, symptoms must be documented so that a third-party reviewer understands their impact on the client. Thus, clinicians must also learn to document onset, frequency, duration, and severity of symptoms, and the resulting functional impairments when recording a client's problem.

MENTAL HEALTH CRITERIA

Relatively few insurance companies clearly depict their criteria for reimbursement for mental health services. Often vague statements are provided, without clear interpretation. Few third-party payors provide examples of what is expected in documentation. There are no clear state requirements, other than from state-funded Medicaid. Medicaid provider manuals range from a few pages to several hundred pages of regulations depending on the state. Some states that license mental health facilities periodically audit charts to monitor the quality of services.

When someone has an auto accident and has insurance coverage to pay for the car being repaired, the insurance company will not accept a bill from the repair shop until evidence of what repairs took place is provided. Their methods of documentation may include photographs of the damage and a detailed list of services that are concordant with acceptable standards. Likewise, when a dentist performs services, X-rays are sent to the insurance company as evidence of the need for services. In the delivery of mental health services, we cannot take photographs or X-rays of the damage, but we can provide written documentation that follows the same general principles.

Third-party payors have various requirements for reimbursement of services from state to state and company to company, but the guidelines are fairly consistent, including:

1. Services must be medically or therapeutically necessary.
2. Services must be directed toward a diagnosable mental illness or disorder.
3. Services must be consistent with the diagnosis and degree of impairment.
4. There must be documentation of reasonable progress consistent with the treatment of the disorder.
5. The treatment plan must include specific discharge criteria written in behavioral terms.
6. Services must be specifically directed toward the diagnosis.
7. To receive continued services, there must be documented evidence of continued impairment.
8. The progress notes must clearly reflect the treatment plan goals and objectives.

Without such criteria, there is no clear means of documenting that the services being rendered are needed. Although third-party payors' specific regulations regarding forms, frequency of reports, and so forth differ, the overall information requested is remarkably similar.

CRITERIA FOR CLINICAL SIGNIFICANCE

The *DSM-IV* (APA, 1994) states:

> The definition of mental disorder in the introduction to *DSM-IV* requires that there be clinically significant impairment or distress. To highlight the importance of considering this issue, the criteria sets for most disorders include a clinical significance criterion (usually worded ". . . causes clinically significant distress or impairment in social, occupational, or other important areas of functioning.") This criterion helps establish the threshold for the diagnosis of a disorder in those situations in which the symptomatic presentation by itself (particularly in its milder forms) is not inherently pathological and may be encountered in individuals for whom a diagnosis of "mental disorder" would be inappropriate. . . ." (p. 7)

The *DSM-IV* suggests it is possible for a person to experience symptoms of a disorder but not be diagnosed as such because symptoms are not severe enough. On the other hand, inadequate documentation can make clients appear to be less afflicted than they actually are. If medical necessity is not found to be evident, due to insufficient or inadequate documentation, reimbursement will be denied. The following examples highlight incidents where medical necessity is not adequately documented:

- *Poorly Documented Symptoms:* "The client is depressed, withdrawn, suffers from lack of sleep and fatigue, feels anxious, and has feelings of confusion."

  Specific Problems: This statement does not provide adequate documentation for a diagnosis because it lists only symptoms. Impairment is not validated. It is possible that the client is functioning adequately because the severity of symptoms is minimal. A normal life stressor could lead to these symptoms. Most people at times experience some degree of these symptoms and are not considered psychopathological.

Properly Documented Example: "The client meets criteria for major depression as evidenced by feeling depressed most of the time for the past two months, withdrawing from almost all people, daily suicidal ideations, sleeping less than three hours per night, physical and mental fatigue, and increased worrying. There is resulting educational and social impairment in that he has not attended college classes in over one month and usually stays in his room by himself, avoiding friends and family."

- *Poorly Documented Example:* "The client has panic attacks."

Specific Problems: This statement also does not provide enough information to warrant a diagnosis of a mental disorder. The label "panic attacks" should be explained in terms of frequency, duration, and severity. Many people have had at least one panic attack in their lives, but it does not constitute a panic disorder. Others have frequent, debilitating panic attacks causing significant dysfunction that interferes with a wide array of daily activities.

Properly Documented Example: "The client is diagnosed with panic disorder without agoraphobia. Panic attacks lasting at least 30 minutes have occurred at least twice per day for the past year. Symptoms are evidenced by palpitations, hot flashes, sweating, chest pains, dizziness, trembling, and fleeing the situation. During the past three months, panic attacks have increased in duration and intensity, resulting in avoiding any new or stressful situations and leaving work early approximately three to four times per week."

- *Poorly Documented Example:* "The client is having trouble coping with a recent divorce and death of a loved one."

Specific Problems: This statement does not justify the need for treatment based on the medical model. These are normal life stressors or events that many people experience, and there is no evidence of abnormal impairments or a need for mental health services. It is expected that a person would have difficulty coping with a recent divorce and the death of a loved one.

Properly Documented Example: "The client is experiencing an adjustment disorder with depressed mood as evidenced by increased depression, withdrawal, and difficulties coping. Symptoms have occurred since the onset of two major stressors in the past three months including the death of his mother and his divorce. Affective impairment is noted as evidenced by feeling dysphoric most of the time and having difficulties feeling motivated to work, shop, or resume usual activities."

- *Poorly Documented Example:* "The client is missing four days of work per week, has no friends, and has not phoned any family members for more than two months."

Specific Problems: In this case, functional impairments may exist, but no mental disorder is documented. The impairment must be the result of a mental disorder to demonstrate medical necessity for receiving mental health treatment. Otherwise, services other than mental health may be needed.

Properly Documented Example: "The client has felt depressed for the past three weeks as evidenced by suicidal ideations, feeling hopeless and worthless, and excessive eating. There is resulting affective, cognitive, educational, and physical impairment as evidenced by constant fatigue, missing school 50% of the time from lack of sleep (average 3 hrs./night), decreased concentration (unable to comprehend after reading more than 3 to 4 minutes at a time), weight gain of 12 pounds in past three weeks, and increased negative self-statements noted by others."

Figure 2.1 provides a helpful format to use when documenting a client's symptoms and resulting impairments or dysfunctions. Documentation procedures that state only whether symptoms exist can be compared to stating that an automobile tire is low on air.

FIGURE 2.1
Suggested Format for Documenting Client Symptoms and Functional Impairments

The client has been experiencing ____(problem area)____ for the past ____(time span)____ as evidenced by ____(list of symptoms which are concordant with DSM-IV)____ , resulting in ____(specific areas of impairment)____ impairment(s) as evidenced by ____(specific examples of functional impairments)____ .

Most automobile tires at some time are low on air. This may be because the automobile has hit a bump, cold weather, or even due to normal wear. Just because a tire is low on air does not always mean the driver cannot drive the car. The severity of the problem depends, in part, on how low on air the tire is. Other descriptors, such as how long there has been trouble with the tire losing air, how often it must be filled up, and the condition of the tire will help you make a more informed decision about whether to continue driving the car or to take it in for service. Likewise, listing mental health symptoms alone does not provide enough specific information to make a diagnosis or plan treatment.

Figure 2.2 illustrates the difference between simply listing a client's symptoms and documenting the impacts of those symptoms

FIGURE 2.2

Two Profiles of Clients Presenting with Major Depression

Profile 1   Listing Symptoms Only

Client A	**Client B**
Depressed mood	Depressed mood
Social withdrawal	Social withdrawal
Suicidal ideations	Suicidal ideations
Lack of pleasure	Lack of pleasure
Poor concentration	Poor concentration
Weight gain	Weight gain

Profile 2   Listing Additional Descriptors for Clients A and B Documents Difference in Diagnosis and Medical Necessity

Client A		**Client B**
Onset:	4 years ago	12 years ago
Frequency:	2 episodes since onset	2-3 episodes/year (cycling)
Duration:	Episodes last ≤ 2 weeks	Episodes last 30-45 days
Severity:	Mild	Severe, occasional psychotic features
Extent of impaired function:	Sometimes late for work	Recently fired from job, 8 job losses, no friends, 4 suicide attempts, 6 hospitalizations for depression, currently in bankruptcy, emerging panic symptoms, gained 35 lbs. in past 6 months
	No job losses	
	Sometimes avoid friends	
	No hospitalizations	
	Gained 10 lbs. in past 6 months	

by adding qualifiers to demarcate additional dimensions of impairment. Profile 1 represents two clients appearing to suffer from the same problem. Notice the difference, however, when further descriptors are added in Profile 2.

Adding descriptors such as onset, frequency, and so on shows that Client B is more severely impaired than Client A. Documentation procedures that address only symptomology miss this important distinction. For this reason it is difficult to make a clear diagnosis when only symptoms are described. Likewise, it is difficult to convince third-party payors that a diagnosis (or treatment) is warranted when only symptoms are documented.

In addition, when documentation of specific functional or behavioral impairment is lacking, there is meager evidence to use in determining the type and number of services most appropriate for the client. The *DSM-IV* (APA, 1994) states, "Making a *DSM-IV* diagnosis is only the first step in a comprehensive evaluation. To formulate an adequate treatment plan, the clinician will invariably require considerable additional information about the person being evaluated beyond that required to make a *DSM-IV* diagnosis" (p. xxv).

Appropriate documentation for diagnosis, treatment planning, and reimbursement requires specifying the degree to which symptoms are impairing various areas of the client's functioning. Current standards in documentation incorporate the level of functional impairment as the measurement standard of the effects of mental illness symptoms. Incorporating impairments and dysfunctions presents a clearer picture of a client's mental status. Also, decisions regarding the medical necessity of treatment are more clearly communicated, and treatment planning may be written and understood more clearly.

FUNCTIONAL IMPAIRMENTS

Functional impairments are significant dysfunctions in daily living, impacting affective, cognitive, occupational, social, or other functioning for which the client needs mental health services (i.e., medical necessity is demonstrated) to adequately return to normal or previous levels of functioning. In other words, without such services, the client is likely to remain dysfunctional. For example, a currently depressed person might have a history of going to work and working productively five days per week. Since the onset of depression, however, the client has been attending work only two to three days per week, resulting in significantly decreased production and is in jeopardy of termination. This same client may also be experiencing increased social withdrawal and avoiding previous friends, thereby cutting off potential social supports. Areas of impairment for this client are described as occupational and social. Other areas of impairment due to depression could exist also, including physical, affective, cognitive impairments, and any other aspect in which a person's activities of daily living are restricted due to a mental disorder. Figure 2.3 provides various examples of functional impairments.

Because current documentation guidelines require providing observable and measurable evidence of changes in functional impairments resulting from treatment, the diagnostic interview should include obtaining baseline measures of the client's degree of functional impairment.

ASSESSMENT PROCEDURES

The initial diagnostic assessment is the backbone of clinical documentation. It provides a clinical history and current snapshot of the purpose for which services are needed. Several aspects of the client's life are reviewed and subsequently integrated in a diagnostic summary that considers a full range of function status. Figure 2.4 lists JCAHO requirements for the initial assessment.

TREATMENT PLANNING

Although the collection of clinical information is ongoing, the information gathered in the initial diagnostic assessment is most crucial because it directly affects the treatment plan, progress notes, and subsequent reports. The treatment plan is based on the diagnostic assessment. All information written in the treatment plan must correspond to the assessment and information gathered in subsequent sessions. That is, targeted issues for treatment should be carefully examined in the intake and subsequent sessions, rather

FIGURE 2.3
Examples of Functional Impairments

Occupational	"Work production for the client has decreased by more than 75% since the death of his spouse, resulting in potential termination if quota is not met by July 10th."
Academic	"Recent school reports indicate that client is angry at classmates, teachers, and family members almost all of the time making it difficult to concentrate on academics. Grades have dropped two letter grades in the past two terms."
Social	"Client has not left her house nor contacted any family members in the past five months, since panic attacks began. Previously client was highly involved socially and with her family."
	"Client is ostracized by classmates due to hyperactivity and immature behaviors on the playground. Frustration, aggressive outbursts, and temper tantrums have increased."
Affective	"Client reports significant sadness, boredom, and grief, resulting in increased suicidal threats."
Physical	"Client reports inability to perform usual activities of daily living, extreme fatigue, increased headaches, loss of 40 lbs. due to low appetite, and dizziness since losing his job."
Combinations	"Client's mother indicates that he is failing in school, has lost all of his friends, has been fired from his job, and has been arrested for marijuana possession for the third time. Before he was injured in the auto accident he received A's and B's in school, seldom missed work, and had no history of drug or alcohol use."

than simply appearing in the treatment plan without written justification that dysfunction exists.

The treatment plan is a dynamic document that is subject to revisions as treatment progresses and more information is learned about the client. A well-formed treatment plan is crucial to ensuring reimbursement for services because it sets the course of therapy. Likewise, properly written progress notes are important because they are the sole source of documentation that treatment plan goals and objectives are being met.

FIGURE 2.4
JCAHO (1997a) Standards for Mental Health Assessment

PE.1	Each individual's physical and psychological status and social functioning are assessed.
PE.1.1	An initial screening and/or assessment of each individual's physical, psychological, and social status is conducted to determine the need for care, the type of care to be provided, and the need for any further assessment.
PE.1.2	The organization has an assessment or screening procedure for the early detection of mental illness that is life threatening, indicates severe personality disorganization or deterioration, or may seriously affect the treatment or rehabilitation process.
PE.1.3	The need for assessing each individual's nutritional status is determined.
PE.1.4	The need for assessing the full range of each individual's functional status is determined.
PE.1.4.1	An assessment of physical functioning is performed for each individual referred for physical rehabilitation services.
PE.1.5	An emotional and behavioral assessment of each individual is completed and entered in the clinical record. The assessment includes at least a history of emotional, behavioral, and substance-abuse problems or treatment, including
PE.1.5.1	use of alcohol and other drugs by family members;
PE.1.5.2	current emotional and behavioral functioning;
PE.1.5.3	maladaptive or problem behaviors;
PE.1.5.4	when indicated, a psychiatric evaluation;
PE.1.5.5	when indicated, a MSE appropriate to the individual's age;
PE.1.5.6	when indicated, a psychological assessment, including intellectual, projective, neuropsychological, and personality testing; and
PE.1.5.7	when indicated, other functional evaluations of language, self-care, visual-motor, and cognitive functioning.
PE.1.6	Assessments identify community resources used by the individual.

(continued)

FIGURE 2.4 (Continued)

PE.1.7	A psychological assessment is completed and entered in the clinical record for each individual.
PE.1.7.1	As appropriate, the psychosocial assessment includes information about the individual's
PE.1.7.1.1	environment and home;
PE.1.7.1.2	leisure and recreation;
PE.1.7.1.3	spirituality;
PE.1.7.1.4	childhood history;
PE.1.7.1.5	military service history;
PE.1.7.1.6	financial status;
PE.1.7.1.7	usual social, peer group, and environmental setting;
PE.1.7.1.8	sexual orientation; and
PE.1.7.1.9	family circumstances.
PE.1.7.2	The psychological assessment includes determining the need for the family's participation.
PE.1.7.3	In the care of a dying individual, the psychological assessment includes the social, spiritual, and cultural variables that influence the perceptions and expressions of grief by the individual or family.
PE.1.8	When appropriate, a vocational assessment is completed and entered in the clinical record.
PE.1.9	When appropriate, an educational assessment is completed and entered in the clinical record.
PE.1.10	When appropriate, a legal assessment is completed and entered in the clinical record.

Note: Additional JCAHO assessment standards deal with client concerns, such as assessment of physical health, laboratory testing, and services to special groups.

THE FINANCIAL IMPACT OF
CLINICAL DOCUMENTATION

In the not-so-distant past, third-party reimbursement for mental health services was virtually guaranteed. Today, however, the quality of documentation directly affects the financial status of the clinic and therapist. The effect of an audit can result, and often has resulted, in therapists facing thousands of dollars in financial penalties to third parties when client charts are not in compliance with accepted standards. Scores of clinics have gone bankrupt because they were unable to return funds to an insurance company after an audit. Keep in mind that paybacks do not always indicate that treatment was unwarranted or that a therapist was unscrupulous. Appropriate treatment can also be penalized as a result of insufficient documentation.

One common auditing procedure incorporated by third-party payors is to audit a set number of charts and use that as the basis for determining what percentage of files at the clinic are not in compliance with documentation procedures. For example, if 100 charts are audited and 20 are determined not to demonstrate medical necessity for services, the insurance company may determine that 20% of all monies it paid to the clinic during the audit period (often three years) must be paid back. In this case, if a clinic employs five therapists who each see an average of 10 patients from the auditor's insurance company per week, the total number of visits would look like this:

5	Therapists
× 10	Clients per week (each)
× 52	Weeks per year
× 3	Years (audit period)
7,800	Client visits reimbursed by the insurance company

This results in a total of 7,800 client visits in the three-year period. If the insurance company reimbursed the clinic $50 per visit, the total payment to the clinic in the three-year period would be $390,000. An audit resulting in 20% noncompliance would suggest a 20% payback totaling $78,000 plus interest! One therapist, at this rate, would owe the insurance company $15,600 for seeing only 10 clients per week from one paying source! Most therapists would have tremendous difficulty paying back such an audit. If the clinic is footing the bill, two usual payback procedures are for the insurance company to deduct payment from its future reimbursements to the clinic or for the clinic to pay back a set amount monthly. Either procedure makes it difficult to meet payroll until the amount is paid off (which often is the time for another audit).

In the event that a clinic will face an audit, there should be clear contractual or employment contract provisions between the clinic and its therapists to determine who is responsible for audit paybacks. When therapists are paid based on a commission of fees received, contracts generally state that the clinician will pay back the income received from the specific files under audit. For example, if the clinician is paid 55% of money received for services, his or her payback amount would be 55% of the total payback for his or her portion of the audit. The procedure is more difficult for clinics that pay therapists salaries because, in most cases, the clinic bears the brunt of the entire payback. Fortunately, clear and thorough documentation drastically reduces the possibility of making paybacks to third parties.

Accurate documentation procedures not only help a clinic remain in business but also provide for clinical and ethical responsibility. They aid in accurate diagnosis, treatment planning, continued demonstration of need for services, and validating the effects of therapy. Documentation skills do not add to the level of paperwork in the therapeutic process. On the contrary, when good documentation procedures are adopted, the time needed to accurately chart a case decreases.

LEGAL ISSUES IN DOCUMENTATION

A major focus in the study of litigation in mental health malpractice has been examining psychological records (Fulero & Wilbert, 1988). Over- and underdocumentation pose different sets of problems. Documenting everything that takes place in treatment may violate the client's confidentiality in areas that are not necessary to document therapeutically, whereas underdocumenting may fail to document that specific services are taking place. In a 1988 study, Fulero and Wilbert found that more than 50% of therapists surveyed withheld nothing in their patients' records. Other therapists endorsed withholding information in patients' records regarding: (a) speculations or opinions, (b) others' names, (c) keep no or minimal records anyway, (d) anything damaging, (e) highly personal information, (f) infidelity, (g) sexual preference or behavior, (h) process notes, (i) diagnostic labels, (j) criminal behaviors, and others.

Soisson, VandeCreek, and Knapp (1987) reviewed cases in which records influenced the outcomes of malpractice suits. They noted that in a malpractice claim, the plaintiff must demonstrate that:

1. The practitioner (defendant) owed a duty to the client (plaintiff) based on an established therapeutic relationship.

2. The quality of care provided by the practitioner fell below the standard of care expected of the average practitioner.

3. The patient suffered or caused harm or injury.

4. The practitioner's dereliction of duty was the direct cause of harm or injury (Cohen, 1979).

The most common grounds for malpractice are identified as:

1. Unauthorized release of information,

2. Negligent treatment of suicidal or aggressive patients,

3. Sexual relations between patient and therapist,

4. Failure to diagnose adequately, and

5. Improper hospitalization of a patient.

In each of these examples, clinical documentation is crucial in the psychotherapist's defense. Specific information in the patient's record may demonstrate that effective therapeutic principles were followed, but the client did not comply or was not honest in the clinical presentation.

In cases of suicide, the practitioner or agency has not been held legally responsible when records indicate that adequate assessment and treatment procedures were conducted (*Dalton v. State,* 1970; *Johnson v. United States,* 1976). Without adequate documentation, the therapist has been held accountable in litigation. Slovenko (1979) states, "an inadequate record of itself is taken to be indicative of poor care." Likewise, adequate records, but with poor follow-up of the clinical observations, may put the therapist in jeopardy.

Gutheil and Appelbaum (1982) state that clinical records should be written from the perspective of future readers. Soisson et al. (1987) suggest that in the case of a suicidal client, documentation should include an assessment of the risk, options considered for the prevention of suicide, and possible treatments (including advantages and disadvantages).

The treatment process is a series of systematic procedures in which most aspects of the client's life are examined in order to rule out specific areas of impairment that might otherwise be overlooked. The biopsychosocial assessment is designed to integrate past and present behaviors. It is the first clinical procedure in the assessment and treatment process.

HIGHLIGHTS
of Chapter 2

★ Clinical skills, in themselves, are not sufficient to obtain extended services for clients when third-party payors are involved. Documentation skills are needed to demonstrate accountability.

★ Graduate school training in mental health services has often assumed that documentation skills are being learned at internship sites, but this may not be the case.

★ Third-party reimbursement generally requires that mental health services be medically necessary for services to be reimbursed.

★ Medical necessity is demonstrated by the existence of a mental health disorder as evidenced by significant functional impairments.

★ Without documentation of functional impairments, it is difficult to assess the need for mental health services.

★ Indicators such as onset, frequency, duration, and severity significantly increase the specificity of documentation of the diagnosis, symptoms, and impairments.

★ Documentation skills can improve with adequate training and simplified procedures.

★ Mental health services from any school of thought can be documented in a measurable manner and in behavioral terms.

★ Poor documentation significantly increases a clinician's chances of being held liable in litigation.

★ Therapists are encouraged to conduct therapy from their choice of schools of thought, but documentation procedures are written according to a medical model in behavioral terms.

3

The Biopsychosocial Assessment

The biopsychosocial assessment provides background information for several areas of the client's life. Much of the information is obtained in the initial interview and additions and revisions are made throughout therapy. Information covered includes biological (or physical), psychological, and social. Biological information includes information about the client's family, development, education, employment, legal, and other medical history. Psychological information focuses on previous and current psychological status and treatment. Social information includes the client's social relationships and supports. Each area of biopsychosocial information collected should include both strengths and weaknesses.

General demographic information, such as number of years of schooling, may be obtained in pre-interview questionnaires. The clinician reviews this information for clinical significance and incorporates it into the assessment and, subsequently, the treatment plan.

It is important to avoid redundancy in the primary information gathering period. Nothing new is learned and time is wasted if the same questions are asked in presession questionnaires, phone screenings, and in the diagnostic assessment interview. Moreover, the client is likely to become frustrated if the initial phone screening, a presession questionnaire, and the clinician solicit the same information. Rather, each method of information gathering should integrate and expand on data already collected. For example, instead of asking about a client's marital status at each stage of information gathering, the initial phone screening might determine the marital status, a presession questionnaire might identify relationship issues, and the clinician might probe stressors, strengths, and dynamics of the relationship (if applicable) in the diagnostic interview.

The diagnostic assessment is *not* designed to be a counseling session. Focusing on counseling during the initial interview may be counterproductive because the time is needed to collect discrete types of information. It is true, however, that a clinician who skillfully conducts the diagnostic interview in both an empathic and professional manner can assure clients that they are understood and allow them to leave the interview ready for treatment. Thus, the diagnostic session may ultimately have the effects of a productive counseling session even though no therapy was offered.

Each piece of information collected in the biopsychosocial assessment possesses clinical significance, but when taken together present a clear clinical picture of the client. At this point, the therapist is no longer dealing with unrelated data but with the whole person in the realm of his or her past and present environment.

CONDUCTING THE BIOPSYCHOSOCIAL ASSESSMENT

Prior to conducting the initial interview, it is necessary to obtain the client's *informed consent*. The therapist should begin by informing the client of the purpose of the interview and how results will be disseminated. Written statements in the initial interview such as, "The client acknowledges and understands the benefits and risks of providing the information requested in this evaluation and has agreed to allow results to be shared with . . . ," document informed consent. Some clinicians have the client sign that they have had the information explained to them.

Just as pre-interview information gathering builds on information gleaned from an initial phone screen or referral, information gathered in the interview should also build on itself. All of the information should be reviewed to produce a diagnosis and subsequent treatment plan. Some clinicians prefer to mail all pre-interview questionnaires to clients and ask them to fill them out prior to the first meeting. Others ask the client to come early to the initial interview to fill out the questionnaires.

Using preformatted questionnaires can save time for the clinician. For example, Figures 3.1 and 3.2 follow similar formats that allow the clinician to more easily access information when writing reports, treatment plans, and reviewing cases. Figure 3.1 provides an example of a client personal history form. Figure 3.2, an example of an initial intake, which also includes biopsycosocial

FIGURE 3.1
Personal History Form

Adult Personal History Form

Case No. _053983D_

Client's Name _John Doe_   Date _5-3-98_

Gender _F_ _✓M_   Date of Birth _2-15-53_   Age _45_

Form completed by (if someone other than client)_____

Address _34567 Main Street_

City _Longview_   State _CA_   Zip _99999_

Phone (Home) _(555)-555-1213_   (Work) _(555) 555-1211_   ext. _9876_

IF YOU NEED ANY MORE SPACE FOR ANY OF THE FOLLOWING QUESTIONS PLEASE USE THE BACK OF THE SHEET

Primary reason(s) for seeking services: __Addictive behavors   __Alcohol/drugs
__Anger management   __Anxiety   __Coping   ✓Depression
__Eating disorder   __Fear/phobias   __Mental confusion   __Sexual concerns
__Sleeping problems   __Other mental health concerns (specify)_____

FAMILY INFORMATION

Relationship	Name	Age	Living Yes	Living No	Living with you Yes	Living with you No
Mother	Debra Doe	X		✓		✓
Father	Robert Doe	X		✓		✓
Spouse	None (1- Deceased 2-Divorced)		①✓	②✓		✓
Children	Cynthia Doe	16	✓			✓
	Victoria Doe	13	✓			✓

Significant Others (Brothers, Sisters, Grandparents, Step-relatives, Half-relatives. Please specify relationship.)

Relationship	Name	Age	Living Yes	Living No	Living with you Yes	Living with you No
Brother	Raymond Doe	48	✓			✓

Page 1

(continued)

FIGURE 3.1 (Continued)

Marital Status   (more than one answer may apply)

__Single   __Divorce in process   __Unmarried, living together
                                       Length of time_____   Length of time_____

__Legally married   __Separated   ✓Divorced
Length of time_____   Length of time_____   Length of time 4 yrs.

✓Widowed   __Annulment
Length of time 10 mos.   Length of time_____   Total number of marriages ____

Assessment of Current Relationship (if applicable)   __Good   __Fair   ✓Poor with ex-wife

Parental Information
✓Parents legally married (now deceased)   __Mother remarried: Number of times_____
__Parents have even been separated   __Father remarried: Number of times_____
__Parents ever divorced

Special curcumstances (e.g. raised by person other than parents, information about spouse/children not living with you, etc.)
_____
_____

DEVELOPMENT

Are there special, unusual, or traumatic circumstances that affected your development: ✓No   __Yes
If Yes, which type(s) of child abuse? __Sexual ✓Physical __Verbal.   Abuse was as __Victim __Perpetrator
Other childhood issues: __Neglect __Inadequate nutrition   __Other (specify)_____
Comments re: Childhood development My father often beat me up when I was a teenager_____
_____
_____

SOCIAL RELATIONSHIPS

Check how you generally get along with other people: (check all which apply)
✓Affectionate   __Aggressive   __Avoidant   __Fight/argue often   __Follower
✓Friendly   __Leader   __Outgoing   ✓Shy/withdrawn   __Submissive
__Other (specify)_____
_____

Sexual Orientation: heterosexual   Comments:_____

Sexual Dysfunctions? ✓No   __Yes (describe)_____

Any current or history of being as sexual perpetrator? ✓No   __Yes (describe)_____
_____

CULTURAL / ETHNIC

From which cultural or ethinic group, if any, do you belong? WASP_____
Are you experiencing any problems due to culturual or ethnic issues? ✓No   __Yes (describe)_____
_____
Other cultural / ethnic information:_____
_____

FIGURE 3.1 (Continued)

SPIRITUAL / RELIGIOUS

How important to you are spiritual matters? __Not __Little __Moderate ✓Much
Are you affiliated with a spiritual or religious group? ✓No __Yes (describe)_____
Were you raised within a spiritual or religious group? __No ✓Yes (describe) **very strict**
Would you like your spiritual/religious beliefs incorporated into the counseling? __No ✓Yes (describe) **I would like honest, ethical practices.**

LEGAL

Current Status
Are you involved in any active cases (traffic, civil, criminal)? __No ✓Yes
If Yes, please describe and indicate the court and hearing/trial dates and charges_____
  Child support hearing in two weeks

Are you presently on probation or parole? ✓No __Yes
If Yes, please describe_____

Past History

Traffic violations	__No ✓Yes	DWI, DUI, etc.	✓No __Yes
Criminal involvement	✓No __Yes	Civil involvement	✓No __Yes

If you responded Yes to any of the above, please fill in the following information.

Charges	Date	Where (city)	Results
Speeding 45 in a 30	1985	Cambridge	Paid Fine

EDUCATIONAL

Fill in all that apply	Years of education 12	Currently enrolled in school ✓No __Yes	
✓High School grad/GED	__Vocational: Number of years_____	Graduated __No __Yes	Major_____
	__College: Number of years_____	Graduated __No __Yes	Major_____
	__Graduate: Number of years_____	Graduated __No __Yes	Major_____

Other training_____
Special circumstances (e.g. learning disabilities, gifted, etc.) **Average grades when in school**

EMPLOYMENT

Begin with most recent job, list job history:

Employer	Dates	Title	Reason left the job	How often miss work?
4M	1987-Present	Miller		lately 2days/wk
Stanford's	1984-1987	Laborer	new Job	seldom
Mengers	1979-1984	Laborer	new Job	seldom
Pollies	1975-1979	Sales	new Job	seldom

Currently: ✓FT __PT __Temp __Laid-off __Disabled __Retired __Social Security __Student
__Other (describe)_____

Page 3

(continued)

FIGURE 3.1 (Continued)

MILITARY

Military experience? __No ✓Yes   Combat experience? ✓No __Yes   Where?_____
Branch **Army**_____   Discharge date__**1975**
Date drafted_____   Type of discharge **honorable**
Date enlisted **1971**_____   Rank at discharge **Sargeant**

LEISURE / RECREATIONAL

Describe special areas of interest or hobbies (e.g., art, books, crafts, physical fitness, sports, outdoor activities, church activities, walking, exercising, diet/health, hunting, fishing, bowling, traveling, etc.)

Activity	How often now?	How often in the past?
Sports events	none	weekly
outdoor activities	seldom	weekly

MEDICAL / PHYSICAL HEALTH

Check all that apply and describe below:

__AIDS	__Constipation	__Hepatitis	__Sore throat
__Alcoholism	__Chicken Pox	__High blood pressure	__Scarlet Fever
__Abdominal pain	__Dental problems	__Kidney problems	__Sinusitis
__Abortion	__Diabetes	__Measles	__Small Pox
__Allergies	__Diarrhea	__Mononucleosis	__Stroke
__Anemia	__Dizziness	__Mumps	__Sexual problems
__Appendicitis	__Drug abuse	__Menstrual pain	__Tonsillitis
__Arthritis	__Epilepsy	__Miscarriages	__Tuberculosis
__Asthma	__Ear infections	__Neurological disorders	__Toothache
__Bronchitis	__Eating problems	__Nausea	__Thyroid problems
__Bed wetting	__Fainting	__Nose bleeds	__Vision problems
__Cancer	✓Fatigue	__Pneumonia	__Vomiting
__Chest pain	__Frequent urination	__Rheumatic Fever	__Whooping cough
__Chronic pain	__Headaches	__SexuallyTransmitted Diseases	__Other (describe)
__Colds/Coughs	__Hearing problems	__Sleeping disorders	

List any current health concerns **low energy**_____

List any recent health or physical changes_____

Nutrition

Meal	How often (times per week)	Typical Foods Eaten	Typical amount eaten	Comments
Breakfast	7 / week	cold cereal	__No __Low ✓Med __High	
Lunch	6 / week	Soup- sandwich	__No __Low __Med ✓High	
Dinner	7 / week	meat-potatoes-veg	__No __Low __Med ✓High	
Snacks	20 / week	Junk food	__No __Low __Med ✓High	high appetite

Current Prescribed Medications	Dose	Dates	Purpose	Side Effects
None				

Current Over-the-counter Med's	Dose	Dates	Purpose	Side Effects
None				

FIGURE 3.1 (Continued)

Are you allergic to any medications or drugs? ✓No __Yes (describe)_____

	Date	Reason	Results
Last physical exam	1996	regular check-up	good health
Last doctor's visit	1994	strep throat	given antibiotic - ok
Last dental exam	1997	regular check-up	no problems
Most recent surgery	none		
Other surgery	none		
Upcoming surgery	none		

Family history of medical problems Mother had thyroid condition._____

_____

_____

Please check if there have been any recent changes in the following
__Sleep patterns   ✓Eating patterns   __Behavior   ✓Energy level
__Physical activity level __General disposition   ✓Weight   __Nervousness / tension

Describe changes in areas in which you checked above Gaining weight from overeating and
underactivity. Low energy: Don't feel like doing things.

CHEMICAL USE HISTORY

	Method of use and amount	Frequency of use	Age of first use	Age of last use	Used in last 48 hours Yes	Used in last 48 hours No	Used in last 30 days Yes	Used in last 30 days No
Alcohol	lite social drinking	Rare	21	45		✓		✓
Barbiturates								
Valium/Librium								
Cocaine/Crack								
Heroin/Opiates								
Marijuana								
PCP/LSD/Mescaline								
Inhalants								
Caffeine								
Nicotine								
Over the counter								
Prescription drugs								
Other drugs								

Substance of preference

1. None_____   3. _____

2. _____   4. _____

(continued)

FIGURE 3.1 (Continued)

Substance Abuse Questions

Describe when and where you typically use substances **Rare social drinking**

Describe any changes in your use patterns **None**

Describe how your use has affected your family or friends (include their perceptions of your use)

Reason(s) for use:

___Addicted   ___Build confidence   ___Escape   ___Self-medication

✓ Socialization   ___Taste   ___Other (specify)

How do you believe your substance use affects your life? **not**

Who or what has helped you in stopping or limiting your use?

Does (Has) someone in your family (present/past) have (had) a problem with drugs or alcohol? ✓No ___Yes (describe)

Have you had withdrawal symptoms when trying to stop using drugs or alcohol? ✓No ___Yes (describe)

Have you had adverse reactions or overdose to drugs or alcohol? (describe) **NO**

Does your body temperature change when you drink? ✓No ___Yes (describe)

Have drugs or alcohol created a problem for your job? ✓No ___Yes (describe)

COUNSELING / PRIOR TREATMENT HISTORY

Information about client (past and present):

	No	Yes	When	Purpose ~~Where~~	Your reaction or overall experience
Counseling/Psychiatric treatment		✓ ✓	1993 age 13	Depression Problems with father	It was helpful. Things got better. Don't remember
Suicidal thoughts/attempts	✓				
Drug/Alcohol treatment	✓				
Hospitalizations	✓				
Involvement with self-help groups (e.g. AA, Al-Anon, NA, Overeaters Anonymous)	✓				

FIGURE 3.1 (Continued)

Information about **family / significant others** (past and present):

	No	Yes	When	Where	Your reaction or overall experience
Counseling/Psychiatric treatment	✓				
Suicidal thoughts/attempts	✓				
Drug/alcohol treatment	✓				
Hospitalizations	✓				
Involvement with self-help groups (e.g. AA, Al-Anon, NA, Overeaters Anonymous)					

Please check behaviors and symptoms that occur to you more often than you would like them to take place:

__Aggression	__Dizziness	__Irritability	__Sleeping problems
__Alcohol dependence	__Drug dependence	__Judgment errors	__Speech problems
__Anger	__Eating disorder	__Loneliness	✓Suicidal thoughts
__Antisocial behavior	__Elevated mood	__Memory impairment	__Thoughts disorganized
__Anxiety	✓Fatigue	__Mood shifts	__Trembling
✓Avoiding people	__Gambling	__Panic attacks	✓Withdrawing
__Chest pain	__Hallucinations	__Phobias/fears	__Worrying
__Cyber addiction	__Heart palpitations	__Recurring thoughts	__Other (specify)
✓Depression	__High blood pressure	__Sexual addiction	
__Disorientation	__Hopelessness	__Sexual difficulties	
__Distractibility	__Impulsivity	__Sick often	

Briefly discuss how the above symptoms impair your ability to function effectively. I don't feel like seeing anybody or going to work. Too many bad things have happened to me. I want to get better.

Any additional information that would assist us in understanding your concerns or problems I feel abandoned by life.

What are your goals for therapy? Feel good about myself

Do you feel suicidal at this time? ✓No __Yes (explain)

FOR STAFF USE

Sigmund Z. Adler, PhD
Therapist's Signature/Credentials   Date 5-3-98

Physician's Comments Have reviewed intake material and agree with treatment considerations and diagnoses. Recommend med referral.

Physical Exam: ✓Required __Not Required

Carl J. Erikson, MD
Physician's Signature and Credentials   Date 5-10-98
Certifies case assignment, level of care and need for exam

Page 7

FIGURE 3.2
Initial Intake Including Biopsychosocial Assessment

Adult Initial Assessment

Client's Name _John Doe_____   Date_____

Starting Time_____ Ending Time_____   Duration_____

Session Type ✓90801 ___Other_____

A. BIOPSYCHOSOCIAL ASSESSMENT

1) Presenting Problem _Depressed mood, fatigue, social withdrawal,_ _____
_____lack of motivation_____
_____
_____

2) Signs and Symptoms (DSM based) . . . . **Resulting in Impairment(s)**
(Include current examples; for treatment planning)   (e.g. social, occupational, affective, cognitive, physical)

The client describes feeling depressed for the past 10 months, Since the
death of his wife, as evidenced by usual dysphoric mood, low motivation,
social withdrawal, decreased concentration, fatigue, and anhedonia. It
has resulted in affective, occupational, and social impairment, as
evidenced by missing 10 days of work in the past month, significantly
decreased production at work, avoiding friends and activities
previously enjoyed on a regular basis, and sitting home most of the time.
_____
_____
_____

3) History of presenting problem

Events, precipitating factors or incidents leading to need for services _Spouse passed away_
10 months ago. Since then symptoms of depression have
increased.
_____

Frequency/Duration/Severity/Cycling of symptoms _Depressed most of the time. Current_
episode is not cyclical. Previously treated for depression in 1993
after divorce.
_____

Was there a clear time when Sx worsened? _Death of spouse_____

Family mental health history _None Known_____
_____
_____

Page 1

FIGURE 3.2 (Continued)

4) CURRENT FAMILY AND SIGNIFICANT RELATIONSHIPS   See Personal History Form

No close family relation

Strengths/ support _____

Stressors/problems _Ex-spouse & children avoid him leading to shame_

Recent changes _2nd spouse died. Was in a functional relationship_

Changes desired _Desires to restore relationship with children and spend more time._

Comment on family circumstances _Feels abandoned by all family, no support_

5) CHILDHOOD / ADOLESCENT HISTORY   See Personal History Form

(Developmental milestones, past behavioral concerns, environment, abuse, school, social, mental health)

Normal developmental milestones. States that he was physically abused as a child. Brief counseling at age 13 dealing with issues with father. Average school grades. Describes his family as "dysfunctional." Parents divorced when he was teenager, stayed with mother.

6) SOCIAL RELATIONSHIPS   See Personal History Form

Currently avoids most people.

Strengths/ support _One close friend_

Stressors/problems _Refusing invitations from friends. Doesn't feel like socializing._

Recent changes _Until depressed was much more active socially_

Changes desired _Increase time with friends_

7) CULTURAL / ETHNIC   See Personal History Form

No significant cultural/ethnic practices

Strengths/ support _N/A_

Stressors/problems _N/A_

Beliefs /practices to incorporate into therapy _No_

8) SPIRITUAL / RELIGIOUS   See Personal History Form

strong fundament Christian beliefs

Strengths/ support _Belief in God as source of strength_

Stressors/problems _Not involved in any activities_

Beliefs /practices to incorporate into therapy _Undecided_

Recent changes _No longer attending church activities_

Changes desired _undecided_

9) LEGAL   See Personal History Form

No criminal history. Minor traffic violation. Upcoming Child Support hearing.

Status/impact/stressors _Much stress over court meeting in 2 weeks._

Page 2

(continued)

FIGURE 3.2 (Continued)

---

10) EDUCATION   See Personal History Form

High school graduate - Average intelligence.

Strengths Would like to take public speaking course someday

Weaknesses None

11) EMPLOYMENT / VOCATIONAL   See Personal History Form

Has worked as laborer most of life   Jobs last 4-10 years

Strengths/support History of stable employment all of life.

Stressors/problems Missing approx. 10 days of work per month. Low production.

12) MILITARY   See Personal History Form

Army 4 years Honorable discharge.

Current impact None Known.

13) LEISURE / RECREATIONAL   See Personal History Form

None at present

Strengths/support History of regular involvement recreationally.

Recent changes Dropped almost all activities since spouse died.

Changes desired Wants to return to previous activities.

14) PHYSICAL HEALTH   See Personal History Form

No Known health problems. Has set up appt for physical and
med eval. No medications.

Physical factors affecting mental condition None Known

15) CHEMICAL USE HISTORY   See Personal History Form and Substance Abuse Addendum

Occasional social drinking. No increase since death of spouse.
No history of CD.

Patient's perception of problem None

16) COUNSELING / PRIOR TREATMENT HISTORY See Personal History Form: Client and Family

Previous diagnosis of "dysthymia" five years ago when receiving marital
counseling. Brief counseling as teenager. 6 months counseling for
depression in 1993. Counseling helpful.

Benefits of previous treatment Returned to premorbid functioning in 6 months.

Setbacks of previous treatment None Known

FIGURE 3.2 (Continued)

B. DIAGNOSTIC INTERVIEW

MOOD   (RULE IN AND RULE OUT SIGNS AND SYMPTOMS: VALIDATE WITH DSM)
Predominant mood during interview___ *Depression* _____

Current Concerns   (give examples of impairments (i), severity (s), frequency (f), duration (d)

Adjustment Disorder (w/in 3 months of Identified stressor, Sx persist < 6 months after stressor, marked distressed)
__Depressed   __Anxiety   __Mixed Anxiety & Depression   __Conduct   __Emotions & Conduct   __Unspecified
Specify disturbance: __Acute (<6 months) ✓Chronic (>6 months)_____
                                                     Criteria not met _____

Impairment(s) _social _occupational/educational _affective _cognitive _other_____

Examples of impairment(s)_____

Major Depression (2 or more wks): ✓Usually depressed or ✓anhedonia. (4+ of following): ✓wght +/- 5%/month, ✓appetite+/-,
__sleep +/-, __psychomotor +/-, ✓fatigue, ✓worthlessness/guilt, ✓concentration, ✓death/suidal ideation.
Other; _crying spells,✓withdrawal, _add'l. sx _____

Impairment(s)✓social ✓occupational/educational ✓affective _cognitive _other_____
Examples of impairment(s) *Avoiding friends, missing work 10 days of past month*
Low production (previously "high producer")
Dysthymia (2 or more years): ✓ depressed most of time. (2+ of following): ✓Low/high appetite or eating, __ In/hypersomnia, ✓low
energy/fatigue, ✓low self-esteem, ✓low concentration/decisions,✓hopelessness. Other *Previous diagnosis of*
dysthymia. Endorses symptoms as occurring since teenager.
Impairment(s) _social _occupational/educational ✓affective _cognitive _other_____
Examples of impairment(s) *Feels sad most of the time* _____

Mania (3+): __Grandiosity, __low sleep, __talkative, __flight of ideas, __distractibility, __goals/agitation, __ excessive pleasure.
           Denies _____
Impairment(s) _social _occupational/educational _affective _cognitive _other_____
Examples of impairment(s)_____

Panic Attacks (4+, Abrupt development of): __palpitations, __sweating, __trembling, __shortness of breath, __feeling of choking,
__chest pain, __nausea, __dizziness, __light-headed, __derealization, __fear of losing control, __fear of dying, __numbness, __chills /hot flashes
           Denies _____
Impairment(s) _social _occupational/educational _affective _cognitive _other_____
Examples of impairment(s)_____

Anxiety (GAD: 3+, most of time, 6 months): __restlessness, __easily fatigued, __concentration, __irritability, __muscle tension, __sleep disturbance
           Denies _____
Impairment(s) _social _occupational/educational _affective _cognitive _other_____
Examples of impairment(s)_____

Other Diagnostic Concerns or Behavioral Issues
(E.g., __Dissociation, __Eating, __Sleep, __Impulse control, __Thought disorders, __Anger, __Relationships, __Cognitive, __Phobias,
__Substance Abuse, __Medical conditions, __Somatization, __Phobias, __Sexual, __PTSD.etc.)
           Denies each _____

Impairment(s) _social _occupational/educational _affective _cognitive _other_____
Examples of impairment(s)_____

USE ADDITIONAL PAPER AS NECESSARY

(continued)

FIGURE 3.2 (Continued)

MENTAL STATUS

(Check appropriate level of Impairment: N/A or OK signifies no known impairment. Comment on significant areas of Impairment.)

APPEARANCE

	N/A or OK	Slight	Moderate	Severe
Unkempt, disheveled	O	●	O	O
Clothing; dirty, atypical	●	O	O	O
Odd phys.characteristics	●	O	O	O
Body odor	●	O	O	O
Appears unhealthy	●	O	O	O

POSTURE

	N/A or OK	Slight	Moderate	Severe
Slumped	O	O	●	O
Rigid, tense	●	O	O	O

BODY MOVEMENTS

	N/A or OK	Slight	Moderate	Severe
Accelerated, quick	●	O	O	O
Decreased, slowed	O	O	●	O
Restlessness, fidgety	●	O	O	O
Atypical, unusual	●	O	O	O

SPEECH

	N/A or OK	Slight	Moderate	Severe
Rapid	●	O	O	O
Slow	O	O	●	O
Loud	●	O	O	O
Soft	O	●	O	O
Mute	●	O	O	O
Atypical (e.g., slurring)	●	O	O	O

ATTITUDE

	N/A or OK	Slight	Moderate	Severe
Domineering, controlling	●	O	O	O
Submissive, dependent	O	O	●	O
Hostile, challenging	●	O	O	O
Guarded, suspicious	●	O	O	O
Uncooperative	●	O	O	O

AFFECT

	N/A or OK	Slight	Moderate	Severe
Inappropriate to thought	●	O	O	O
Increased lability	●	O	O	O
Blunted, dull, flat	O	●	O	O
Euphoria, elation	●	O	O	O
Anger, hostility	●	O	O	O
Depression, sadness	O	O	●	O
Anxiety	●	O	O	O
Irritability	●	O	O	O

PERCEPTION

	N/A or OK	Slight	Moderate	Severe
Illusions	●	O	O	O
Auditory hallucinations	●	O	O	O
Visual hallucinations	●	O	O	O
Other hallucinations	●	O	O	O

COGNITIVE

	N/A or OK	Slight	Moderate	Severe
Alertness	●	O	O	O
Attn. span, distractibility	O	●	O	O
Short-term memory	●	O	O	O
Long-term memory	●	O	O	O

JUDGMENT

	N/A or OK	Slight	Moderate	Severe
Decision making	●	O	O	O
Impulsivity	●	O	O	O

THOUGHT CONTENT

	N/A or OK	Slight	Moderate	Severe
Obsessions/compulsions	●	O	O	O
Phobic	●	O	O	O
Depersonalization	●	O	O	O
Suicidal ideation	O	●	O	O
Homicidal ideation	●	O	O	O
Delusions	●	O	O	O

Estimated level of intelligence __Average__

Orientation ✓Time ✓Place ✓Person **x 3**

Able to hold normal conversation? ✓Yes ___No

Eye contact __Normal__

Level of Insight
___Complete denial   ___Slight awareness
___Blames others   ___Blames self
___Intellectual insight, but few changes likely
✓Emotional insight, understanding, change can occur

Patient's view of actions needed to change __increase__ __social & recreational activities__

Comments

No evidence of thought disorder. Appeared depressed. Cried a few times during the interview. He describes his depression as similar to past episode which was alleviated in about 6 months. Good prognosis

FIGURE 3.2 (Continued)

C) DIAGNOSIS VALIDATION

DIAGNOSIS 1 <u>Major Depressive Disorder</u>   Code <u>296.31</u>

DSM Criteria

<u>Depressed most of time past 10 months, significant weight gain,</u>
<u>high appetite, often fatigued, feelings of worthlessness, decreased</u>
<u>concentration, suicidal ideations</u>

Examples of impairment/dysfunction <u>Missing 10 days month at work</u>
<u>Social: avoiding most people.   Affective: usually sad</u>
Additional Validation (e.g. testing, previous records, self report) <u>No testing</u>

DIAGNOSIS 2 <u>Dysthymia Disorder</u>   Code <u>300.4</u>

DSM Criteria

<u>Usually depressed most of life. History of poor appetite, low energy,</u>
<u>low self esteem, feelings of hopelessness</u>

Examples of impairment/dysfunction <u>Feels "blue" most of the time since</u>
<u>teenager</u>
Additional Validation (e.g. testing, previous records, self report) <u>Previous diagnosis of</u>
<u>dysthymia</u>

DIAGNOSIS 3 _____ Code_____

DSM Criteria

_____

_____

_____

Examples of impairment/dysfunction_____

Additional Validation (e.g. testing, previous records, self report)_____

Page 6

(continued)

FIGURE 3.2 (Continued)

Integrated Summary

Clinical Assessment / Diagnostic Summary

(Evaluate, integrate and summarize the following information: Background, medical, social, presenting problem, signs & symptoms and impairments. Tie these in with the patient's strengths and needs. Integration of data is more important than specific details.)

The client describes feeling depressed for the past 10 months, since the death of his wife, as evidenced by usual dysphoric mood, low motivation, social withdrawal, decreased concentration, fatigue, and anhedonia. It has resulted in affective, occupational, and social impairment, as evidenced by missing 10 days of work in the past month, significantly decreased production at work, avoiding friends and activities previously enjoyed on a regular basis, and sitting home most of the time.

He has a history of being prone to depression when under significant stress. Previous counseling has been beneficial. Was given a diagnosis of Dysthymia in 1993. Some counseling as a child.

Some history of physical abuse as a child and marginal dysfunction in the family relationship. He has a previous diagnosis of Dysthymia. Strengths include spiritual beliefs, a premorbid functioning level of high work production and vocational consistency. He desires to return to previous functioning. Weaknesses are in his current level of motivation which is impairing several areas in his life. He describes his family is marginally supportive, at most. Prognosis is good due to his desire to improve, high insight, and previous successful psychotherapy.

	Diagnosis	Code
Axis I	Major Depressive Disorder	296.31
	Dysthymic Disorder	300.04
Axis II	No diagnosis	071.09
Axis III	Defer to Physician	
Axis IV	Occupational problems, economic stress, relationship conflicts	
Axis V	Current GAF = 63	

Sigmund Z. Adler, PhD   5-17-98

Therapist's Signature and Credentials   Date

information, is a report the therapist fills out after collecting sufficient information from the client. Some clinicians do not formally conduct a biopsychosocial assessment but prefer a structured or unstructured initial interview. There are no universally accepted formats for documenting a biopsychosocial assessment, but several exist commercially and in various texts. *The Clinical Documentation Sourcebook,* 2nd edition (Wiger, 1999) provides 36 mental health forms, examples of how to effectively fill them out, and a computer disk to aid in the documentation process.

There are three commonly accepted steps for conducting a biopsychosocial assessment:

1. Determining the presenting problem,
2. Recording the history, and
3. Assessing client strengths and limitations.

After the information is gathered, it should be written up in a psychological report of the problem.

STEP ONE: Presenting Problem (Signs and Symptoms)

The presenting problem is the client's description of the problem rather than the clinician's diagnostic statement of it. It is recorded in the section of the psychological report labeled, "Signs and Symptoms." Although the terms *signs* and *symptoms* are generally combined or used synonymously, the *DSM-IV* (APA, 1994) defines signs as "an objective manifestation of pathological condition. Signs are observed by the examiner rather then reported by the affected individual," whereas symptoms are defined as "a subjective manifestation of a pathological condition. Symptoms are reported by the affected individual rather than observed by the examiner."

The clinician elicits symptoms from the client, including descriptors such as onset, frequency, and so on, and notes the resulting impairments in an effort to both determine the appropriate diagnosis and demonstrate medical necessity for services. The presenting problem should be reflected in the treatment plan; however, this may not be possible when the client is in denial or noncompliant. Clinical noncompliance is especially difficult in cases of third-party reimbursement. Chapter 7 discusses documentation for the noncompliant client.

Throughout this book we'll follow John Doe, a client with depression, through the course of therapy to illustrate the proper documentation process at each stage. Additional case examples will further illustrate correct and incorrect documentation techniques.

(Presenting Problem and Signs)   The first step in the diagnostic intake session is to determine the client's presenting problem and record signs and symptoms.

THERAPIST: What brings you here today?
JOHN DOE (Client): I've been feeling down lately.

(Clarification)   If the presenting problem is unclear, the therapist should seek clarification.

T: Tell me what you mean by "feeling down."
JD: I feel like no one cares about me, I'm sad, and I don't want to go to work anymore.

(Onset)   Next, the therapist determines the onset of the problem.

T: How long have you been feeling this way?
JD: I've been just fine all of my life, but since last year (10 months ago) I have no motivation.

(Antecedents)   The therapist should also investigate whether a specific event (antecedent) occurred that brought on the presenting problem.

T: Did something happen last year?
JD: Yes, my wife died, and I just can't function at work or socially.

(Specific Examples of Impairments)   Once the presenting problem is determined, the therapist should find out how the problem is impairing the client's normal functioning.

T: How has this affected your performance at work?
JD: Over the past several months I keep missing more and more work. I'm now on probation and could lose my job if I don't improve. My production is the lowest in my department.

T: How many days of work have you missed this month?

JD: At least ten.

T: What were your reasons for missing work?

JD: I just didn't feel like getting up, I have no motivation . . . I have no energy, so I called in sick or made something up.

T: Is there anything you enjoy doing at this time?

JD: No, nothing is pleasurable.

(Frequency)   It is necessary at this point for the therapist to determine how frequently the problem occurs or impacts the client's functioning.

T: How often do you feel depressed?

JD: I'm depressed almost all of the time. Seldom a day goes by in which I'm not sad all day long. I just can't think straight or keep my mind on things.

(Comparison to Premorbid Functioning)   Finally, the therapist must inquire and compare the client's current state to premorbid functioning to determine a baseline for treatment.

T: How were things at work for you before your wife died?

JD: It was hard, but I did as well as anyone else, I seldom missed any work, and I was up for a promotion because of seniority.

T: Describe your social life before your wife passed away.

JD: I was outgoing. I went out with friends at least twice a week and loved to play on sports teams at least one time every week.

T: What is currently happening in your life socially?

JD: I sit home alone every evening and weekend. I avoid people at work and cringe at the thought of having to be with people.

T: Are there any other areas in which your life has changed in the past 10 months?

JD: No, that's about it.

The following example illustrates poor documentation of John Doe's signs and symptoms discussed in the diagnostic assessment interview:

> Client is feeling down. Missing work. Few activities. Wife died. Problems at work.

This statement summarizes the topics and current stressors discussed during the intake session but does not demonstrate medical necessity for treatment. Mental health concerns are implied but not documented. In this instance, the vagary of the documentation rather than the therapist's ability will ultimately jeopardize the client's chances of receiving mental health services when the therapist petitions for pre-authorization for treatment. Even if the client receives services, the therapist might ultimately wind up repaying the insurance company the cost of service if audited. A case manager or an auditor does not have access to a session transcript to review the many concerns brought up in the interview. In this case, in a short time period, the therapist adequately solicits the information needed to validate medical necessity for services; however, due to poor documentation skills, there is no evidence of significant impairment to functioning.

Do not blame the auditor or case manager for denying services for a needy client if the documentation does not clearly portray the medical necessity for services. Clients in need of mental health treatment are best served by a therapist who can both deliver quality mental health services and document the scope of services.

The next example provides better documentation for John Doe's problem but still does not clearly describe the medical necessity for treatment:

> Client claims to feel depressed since death of spouse last year. Is not performing adequately at work. No current friendships.

Although this example somewhat documents areas of impairment (affect, occupational, and social), it does not provide diagnostic information concordant with the interview narrative. For example, it is expected that a person would feel depressed after the death of a spouse as part of the normal grieving process; however, John Doe's level of depression is more severe than this documentation suggests. Stating that a person has no current friendships might hint at social concerns but in itself does not provide evidence for medically necessary treatment.

The following example illustrates the proper documentation of John Doe's signs and symptoms. It identifies stressors, time periods, symptoms, and impairments noted in the interview. It also provides baseline data for later assessments of the effects of treatment. Taken together, these signs and symptoms suggest that treatment is medically necessary to restore John Doe to normal functioning:

> The client describes feeling depressed for the past 10 months, since the death of his wife, as evidenced by usual dysphoric mood, low motivation, social withdrawal, decreased concentration, fatigue and anhedonia. It has resulted in affective, occupational, and social impairment as evidenced by missing 10 days of work in the past month, significantly decreasing production at work, avoiding friends and activities previously enjoyed on a regular basis, and sitting home most of the time.

This portion of the diagnostic interview does not go so far into depth as to rule out specific disorders but instead focuses on signs and symptoms of the presenting problem. The presenting problem supplies baseline information that provides initial direction for the diagnostic interview. Further evidence of specific issues, personality disorders, and other concerns will be elicited later in the interview. As well, additional diagnostic information will continue to be formulated throughout therapy.

STEP TWO: History of Present Illness

The client's personal history provides valuable information to help predict future performance, identify precipitating factors such as strengths and stressors that tend to alleviate or increase problem areas, consider previous mental and physical health diagnoses, and recognize behavior patterns. Information may come from a variety of sources and draw from several domains in the client's life. Regulatory agencies, such as JCAHO, require that the assessment process address a number of areas (Figure 3.3).

In addition to recording this information, the therapist documents how these areas are impacting the client's current functioning. The information is directly integrated into the treatment plan and incorporated into therapy. Figure 3.4 describes the type of information that should be elicited and demonstrates its clinical significance.

The following dialogue between John Doe and his therapist demonstrates how to elicit from a client specific information related to the domain areas specified in Figure 3.3 to use in treatment planning. It defines measurable behaviors that both John

FIGURE 3.3

Domain Areas Required to Be Investigated in Biopsychosocial Assessment

Family and Significant Relationships	Military
Childhood and Adolescent History	Leisure/Recreational
Social Relationships	Physical Health
Cultural/Ethnic	Chemical Use
Spiritual/Religious	Counseling/Prior Treatment
Legal	History
Employment/Educational	

Doe and the therapist view to be helpful in restoring and maintaining appropriate mental health. The therapist does not provide therapy at this point, but rather identifies target information for future sessions and current diagnostic significance.

Family and Significant Relationships

T: Tell me about your family.

JD: Since my wife died . . . my second wife . . . I haven't been in contact with her family. I have two children from my first marriage, but they live with their mother.

T: How about your immediate family?

JD: They moved across the country a few years ago. They can't afford to visit me. The last time I saw them was at the funeral. We've never been that close, though.

T: Do you have any friends here?

JD: I see one of my high school friends about once every month or two.

T: When you need to talk to someone about personal issues, who is available or with whom do you feel comfortable?

JD: Certainly not my first wife. She has always poisoned our two children against me so much that they don't even want to visit me on weekends. My ex-wife digs it in that I'm depressed and not a good example for the children.

T: Do you have any relatives you can talk to?

JD: Sometimes I phone my brother in Detroit to complain about things, but he seems to side with my ex-wife. They used to date. I think they're still in touch.

T: What about your friend?

FIGURE 3.4

Type of Information Solicited for Biopsychosocial Domains and Its Clinical Signficance

Solicited Information	Clinical Significance
Strengths/supports	Incorporate into treatment plan to most effectively integrate client's existing strengths and supports available from a wide range of areas.
Stressors/problems	Identify current problem areas that may be contributing to the client's mental health issues; also important diagnostically to justify an adjustment disorder.
Recent changes	Change in itself, whether viewed as positive or negative, often results in a stressful reaction. Note the client's reaction to changes and the permanence of the changes.
Changes desired	Document in the objectives section of the treatment plan and implement using various intervention techniques.
Specific beliefs or practices	Cultural, ethnic, and religious beliefs and practices should be identified prior to beginning treatment. Lack of knowledge in these areas is usually counterproductive, especially when counseling practices might contradict deep-rooted systems or beliefs.
Development —Past behavioral concerns —Past abuse —School issues —Social information —Mental health —Family dynamics	The clinical use of previous history is important because it may provide clues as to the etiology of current behaviors, responses, coping mechanisms, strengths, and disabilities. It helps the therapist to understand difficult developmental issues affecting current behaviors. Much of this information can be obtained from documents filled out by the client prior to the intake session.

JD: Our relationship is mainly competitive . . . you know . . . like playing pool and shooting hoops. Lately, though, I've canceled our engagements. When we're together we want to have fun. If we talked about problems it would take away from the escape.

T: So are you saying that being with your friend helps on another level?

JD: What do you mean?

T: It sounds like being with him is a helpful escape from your problems.

JD: I never thought of it that way . . . yes.

T: Tell me more about how your children impact or affect your mood?

JD: I just feel lower and lower. I sit home and mope and feel so bad that I'm embarrassed to see the children. I used to take them at least two places every week. It's not happening. Nothing good is happening with my family. I have a dead wife, an ex-wife and an ex-family.

T: It sounds like things used to be much better. What changes would you like to see in your relationships?

JD: If I could change anything it would be to have fun with my children.

T: How much time do you now spend with your children?

JD: About two hours a week when they want to see me.

T: How much time would you like to spend with them?

JD: At least ten hours a week, doing things we used to do. I have liberal visitation rights . . . at least on paper.

T: What about your relationships with other people in your life?

JD: I would like to spend more time with my best friend. Things always feel better when we go out and spend time together. It takes my mind off of things.

T: How often do you see him now?

JD: Not in the last three months.

T: How often would you like to see your friend?

JD: At least once or twice a month.

Childhood and Adolescent History

T: Tell me about your childhood.

JD: For the most part it was fairly routine. My parents got along about half the time. I had friends and did well in school. I never got in trouble with the law or in school.

T: Did you ever see a counselor or have any emotional or behavioral problems when you were a child or adolescent?

JD: Well, once when I was about 13 I threatened suicide when my father punished me for something I didn't do.

T: Go on.

JD: My father always accused me of not being obedient and then beat me. He did this several times when I was younger. My mother eventually kicked him out of the house. After that our home life was stable.

T: You mentioned threatening suicide.

JD: I was so stressed out that I didn't feel I could go on any longer. School was getting to be too difficult, I hated my father, and my friends made fun of me because they often heard my parents fighting. I just wanted to give up. I really wouldn't have killed myself, but I didn't want to be around, either. My mother took me to a counselor and after about two or three months I felt better.

T: How has handling change been for you at other times?

JD: Actually, I've never been good at changes. I usually get depressed and isolate myself. I don't like challenges. I like feeling comfortable and secure.

T: How was your school and social life as a child?

JD: I always had friends. People treated me okay, especially after my father left. Things were then more calm at our house. I had average grades in school. It was okay.

Social Relationships

T: Tell me about your social life.

JD: What social life? I have none.

T: Are you presently involved in any activities or see any other people than those you mentioned?

JD: No, not really. I don't feel like it.

T: How long has it been since you did any socializing?

JD: Not since my wife died. Most of our friends were married, now we have nothing in common.

T: Is there anything you miss about being with people or going out?

JD: I used to like just talking to people, I was a real people person. I could talk to anybody. But, it's like I forgot how or have no motivation to do it.

T: How would you like things to be?

JD: I guess if things were better, I'd like to be involved in some sort of recreational activity but not now.

Cultural/Ethnic

T: Do you have any cultural or ethnic beliefs or practices which would be helpful for me to know or which would be helpful to the counseling processes?

JD: No, not really . . . I'm a White, middle-class, Anglo-Saxon Protestant.

Spiritual/Religious

T: Are there any spiritual or religious beliefs that would be helpful for me to know?

JD: Yes, I am a born-again Christian. I always pray before I make a major decision. I was raised with very strict rules of conduct and do not want any advice in counseling that would violate biblical principles.

T: Could you give me an example of what you mean?

JD: Sure, I don't believe in premarital sex; therefore, I hope you don't say I should seek sexual fulfillment in that manner. But, at the same time, I believe that there is strength available from God if I put him first in my life and read positive passages from the Bible.

T: Tell me more about how the spiritual aspects of life can be positive for you.

JD: Although I haven't been to church since she died, I believe that Christians can help and support each other. I used to be very involved in church, but stopped going when she died.

T: Do you think that this could be another avenue to help you at this time?

JD: I don't know if I'm ready yet.

T: What changes, if any, would you like to see in this area?

JD: Well, I used to feel more inner peace when I went to church. I don't want to talk about this now.

Legal

T: Are there any current legal concerns affecting you in any way?

JD: No, I've never been arrested for anything other than minor traffic violations.

T: Is there any court involvement at all at this time?

JD: Well, yes, I'm going through some child-support battles. We will go to court again in about two weeks.

T: How is this affecting you?

JD: Every day it annoys me. I can't afford the amount of support she is asking for. I feel like when I go to work my check is totally to pay for a house I no longer live in. So why should I even go to work? It's not fair at all. I'm still paying for funeral expenses. How can I have a life if all I do is pay money to my ex-wife to support children who don't even want to visit me?

T: It sounds like you are really frustrated about this.

JD: Yes . . . there is no room for me anymore. I can't do anything . . . it's like they own me, and the law is on their side.

Employment/Educational

T: You said before that you have been missing a lot of work. Tell me more about it.

JD: I just have no motivation to go to work. Nothing is satisfying anymore. I used to be a top producer, but now it just doesn't matter because I have no reason to get ahead. The more I make the more my ex-wife gets and the more frustrated I become. Most of the time I'm just too down to feel like I'd be any good at work. What good could I do at work if I can't produce? I guess I'm just a loser, what else can I say?

T: What do you want it to be like at work?

JD: I wish that things were like the way they were before. I made good money . . . I was needed . . . I had goals . . . I never missed work. I really want to be that way again. That's why I'm here. I need a boost.

T: Are there any changes you would like to see educationally?

JD: I have always wanted to take a course in public speaking, but believe me, I'm in no mood right now to do that . . . maybe someday.

T: Someday?

JD: Yes, when I feel better about life.

Military

T: I see on your Personal Information Form that you were in the military. How was it for you?

JD: It was a learning experience. I did my time and survived. I didn't see any action. It was a job. It paid for my schooling. No problems.

Leisure/Recreational

T: What sort of things do you do for fun?

JD: Well, right now just about nothing, anymore.

T: Anymore?

JD: I used to be involved in plenty of activities.

T: Tell me about them.

JD: Okay. My second wife, the one who died, and I used to go to at least one sports event every two weeks and we went to one cultural event every two weeks. The sports were for me and the culture was for her. Actually, after a while we began to enjoy things together.

T: It sounds like you used to be pretty active in a number of areas.

JD: That's right . . . I used to be.

T: Tell me some more of the activities you used to like.

JD: Golfing, bowling, football games, basketball, antique stores, concerts, and going for walks.

T: That's quite a list. Do you miss some of them now?

JD: I do, but I always did them with her. About the only fun I have is with my best friend now and then.

Physical Health

T: How is your physical health?

JD: Oh, it's always been pretty good . . . lately I've felt fatigued, but I'm pretty healthy.

T: When was your last physical or visit to the doctor?

JD: About two years ago I had a physical for work. Everything was fine.

T: Do you have a history of any physical problems?

JD: No, I've always been in good health.

T: How about your family, such as your parents, siblings, or grandparents?

JD: Well, my father and grandmother had some thyroid problems, but I don't know too much about it. Overall, we're a pretty healthy family.

Chemical Use

T: Do you use alcohol or any other drugs?

JD: Yes, I drink socially on occasion, but it is not a problem.

T: How often is that?

JD: Oh, I might drink a few beers once every few months.

T: How does it affect you, or why do you drink?

JD: Just to fit in socially. I don't even enjoy the taste, especially.

T: When did you have your last drink?

JD: About six months ago. I had one glass of wine at an office party.

T: Have you ever had any problems with alcohol or any other drugs?

JD: No, I've never even been drunk. I've never tried any other street drugs.

T: Is there any chemical abuse history in your family?

JD: Not that I know of.

Counseling/Prior Treatment History

T: I noticed on your information form that you were in counseling about fives years ago. Tell me about it.

JD: Well, I saw Dr. Anderson about five years ago for depression after my first wife and I were talking about a separation. It was similar to now. I just had no motivation to do anything, and I started missing work. Also, I already told you about some counseling as a teenager.

T: How did the therapy work out?

JD: We met every week for about six months. About half the time my wife attended the sessions. She suggested that I visit the psychiatrist for medications, but I was afraid to so I didn't. Toward the end of counseling things seemed to get back to normal in our marriage, and I stopped missing work.

T: Was there anything in the counseling that was especially helpful?

JD: I don't remember the specifics, but Dr. Anderson often suggested things we could work on together to help the relationship. It seemed to work . . . at least for a few years.

T: Do you remember if a diagnosis was given?

JD: I believe she said "Dysthymia" or something like that.

T: Later, we'll go over this and see how it relates to you today. It would be helpful if we could write to Dr. Anderson for your previous counseling records. Would that be all right?

JD: Sure.

T: Tell me about the other time you were in counseling.

JD: Like I mentioned before, I went to counseling at age 13 because I had to please my father. You know, it made me appear as the sick person, instead of him.

T: Do you think it was helpful being there?

JD: No, not then, but counseling was okay when I went in 1993.

Interview information can be the most important data available to the clinician. Therefore the quality of the information and how it is used is crucial to the assessment and treatment plan process.

STEP THREE: Client Strengths and Limitations

Throughout the entire interview, client strengths and weaknesses are assessed. JCAHO requires that this information be incorporated into the treatment plan. The previous interview questions can help a therapist document client strengths and weaknesses so that they can be incorporated into counseling (Figure 3.5).

Although specific strengths and weaknesses may not be written directly in the treatment plan, the plan reflects these capabilities in order to provide more efficacious treatment. For example, if a client has good insight, the therapist might consider using insight-oriented therapy in treatment. On the other hand, if a client has severe cognitive deficits but responds well to specific, concrete behavioral intervention, behavior therapy could be more fitting. Clients with supportive social contacts would most likely respond

FIGURE 3.5
Documenting John Doe's Strengths and Weaknesses

Strengths	*Weaknesses*
Recreational activities with best friend take his mind off problems	Little family contact
	His children avoid him
Motivated to increase time with others	Childhood relationship problems with father
History of having friendships	
Strengths in religious/spiritual beliefs	History of difficulty coping with change
Law abiding	Little/no social life at this time
History of stable work record	Stressed due to upcoming court visit (child support)
History of good physical health	
No history of chemical dependency	Missing much work lately
Successful counseling in past	Current low energy
Good insight	Low motivation

FIGURE 3.6
Examples of Areas of Client Strengths or Limitations That
May Be Incorporated into the Treatment Plan

Social

Accepts feedback	Helpful
Accepts responsibility for own behavior	Impulse control
Appropriately accesses support system	Listens to others
Articulate	Maintains appropriate boundaries
Assertive	Makes own decisions
Aware of impact on others	Organization membership(s)
Congruent	Outgoing
Dependable	Respectful
Empathic	Sense of humor
Establishes appropriate boundaries	Sensitive
Friendly	Sharing
Fun-loving	Supports others
Genuine	Tolerant of others
Good hygiene	Willing to please
Has long-term relationships	

Occupational/Educational

Abstract thinker	Good follower
Adapts to changes	Good leader
Articulate	Hard worker
Assertive	Independent
Attention span good	Learns fast
Aware of impact on others	Logical
Bright	Organized
Common sense good	Reads well
Concentration	Reliable
Concrete thinking	Stable employment
Cooperative	Team player
Creative	Uses lists
Dedicated	Willing to please
Dependable	Works hard
Goal focused	Writes well

Affective

Accepts feelings in self	Empathic
Accepts feelings in others	Expresses emotions
Aware of feelings	Integrates thinking and feeling
Aware of impact of feelings on behavior	Range of feelings available
Emotions appropriate	Tolerates emotional discomfort

(continued)

FIGURE 3.6 (Continued)

Cognitive

Abstract thinker	Insight into own behavior
Attention/concentration	Insight into others' behaviors
Aware of how thoughts affect feelings	Intelligent
Aware of how thoughts affect behaviors	Logical
Clear imagery	Memory
Creative	Positive self-dialogue
Delays decision making	Reality testing intact
Flexibility in thinking	Reflects on own behavior

Physical

Eats well	Healthy
Endurance	Maintains normal weight
Exercises regularly	Solid sleep

Note: Provided by Danielle Jordan, PhD. MN School of Professional Psychology.

well to incorporating this support into the treatment, whereas someone with a social phobia might panic if others were included immediately.

Information about client strengths and limitations may be solicited from a variety of sources including observations, questioning during the interview, prediagnostic questionnaires, collateral information, such as reports from other providers or family members, or psychological testing. Knowledge of the client's strengths and weaknesses, as with most clinical information, increases with time and rapport and may be incorporated into treatment throughout the course of therapy. Figure 3.6 lists categories similar to *DSM-IV*'s examples of impairments and represents common strengths and limitations to consider during treatment planning.

The Psychological Report

The psychological report (see example in Appendix A), also known as an integrated summary, a psychological evaluation, a consultative examination, or a clinical assessment, provides a technically accurate yet concise overview of the client's psychological functioning. The psychological report integrates all aspects of the information collected during pre-interview screening and the initial intake. Although several different psychological report formats exist, it is crucial that reports be easily understood by both mental health professionals and non-clinicians (e.g., third-party reviewers).

Different readers focus on different aspects of the report depending on their level of understanding and reason for reading the report. Some readers focus on raw data and observations, whereas others prefer reading the diagnosis and recommendations. Overall, the report should be written so that the client can understand it; however, the report should also provide enough details to portray an accurate clinical picture. Using technical jargon is unnecessary, especially because the report is meant to be summative. There are at least five sources for integrating information into the psychological report, including:

1. Biographical information collected from pre-interview screening such as information gathered in forms or telephone prescreening.

2. Information from other professionals who have treated the client.

3. Observations made during the initial interview.

4. Test results.

5. Information from collaterals such as significant others, teachers, bosses, friends, or family members.

Effective writing skills are necessary to clearly integrate the several sources of raw data. In addition, reporting raw data from tests or observations is meaningless without interpretation. Consider the difference between the following two statements:

1. "The client's MMPI-2 score indicated elevated scores in the 2, 4, and 7 scales."

2. "The client's MMPI-2 score suggested concerns with depression, anger, and anxiety. People with similar profiles tend to have behavior cycles of acting out, guilt, and subsequent depression."

Although the first statement might be significant to someone trained in using the MMPI-2, the second statement is understandable even to those not trained in clinical interpretation. Some clinicians include both types of statements by listing technical data under Testing and interpreting the data in the report's Summary section.

Factors influencing the report's format include its purpose (the referral question), the writer's theoretical orientation, the intended audience, and writing style. The same writer will often write reports that look different depending on the purpose for which the report will be used. For example, if a report is primarily intended for the parent of a client to read, it will most likely be summative, rather than providing extensive test results or uninterpreted data. A report that is written for professionals may contain extensive clinical nomenclature. This text is not concerned about the particular format used to write the report; rather, it focuses on how to properly document information included in the report.

Psychological reports also vary in length. If a clinician includes all of the information gathered about a client, the report could easily reach 10 to 20 pages. Clinicians who provide little technical information and instead focus on integrating results could produce a report of only a few pages. This author suggests providing adequate details pertaining to the referral question and summarizing other areas. For example, some clinicians administer a standard test battery to every client as a screening process. If the referral question is, "Does this person qualify for an anger management group?" it may not be important to extensively interpret intellectual tests. But, in the case of a brain injury, the interpretation of these tests may be extremely important.

Often the clinician decides which specific tests and procedures to administer after sufficient rule-in/rule-out questions (described in Chapter 5) have been answered and a clearer clinical picture is presented.

Diagnostic and biopsychosocial information continues to be collected and revised throughout the course of therapy and adjustments to the treatment plan made as needed. Some clinicians prefer to wait a few weeks before filling out a biopsychosocial report until they have received adequate collateral information and have attained sufficient information in the sessions. Once the initial biopsychosocial assessment is complete, the next step in the initial intake is to conduct a mental status exam. Chapter 4 introduces several components that can be used to determine a client's current mental state.

HIGHLIGHTS
of Chapter 3

* The biopsychosocial assessment provides historical information from several areas of a client's life. Both strengths and weaknesses are incorporated into treatment planning.

* Biopsychosocial information may be gathered from several sources including questionnaires, clinical questioning, and collateral information.

* Although the purpose of the diagnostic interview is to gather information, it can be both informative and therapeutic by increasing client insight due to the nature of the questions and answers.

* The documentation of both signs and symptoms provides current information regarding mental health symptoms from the client's and therapist's perspective.

* The only clinical information available to a third-party auditor or case manager is that which is furnished by the therapist, therefore inadequate documentation will result in denial of services.

* The best predictor of future behavior is past behavior.

* Assessing client strengths and weakness helps determine which types of interventions may be the most appropriate.

4

The Mental Status Exam

The mental status exam (MSE) is part of the diagnostic interview, and it is administered by both asking questions and making observations. Whereas the biopsychosocial assessment primarily focuses on history, the MSE objectively focuses on the client's current mental state. It includes making several observations about the client designed to clarify and validate clinical information received by other means. It was adapted from the physical examination, which reviews major organ systems, in that it reviews major psychiatric functions. Several MSE formats, such as the Mini Mental Exam (Folstein, Folstein, & McHugh, 1975), are widely used. In general, the greater degree of mental impairment, the more focus the MSE receives. That is, if a client's concerns are more behavioral or affective, the MSE may not reveal any specific mental status issues other than current affective state. But clients presenting with severe psychotic concerns may readily show mental status concerns. It is not common to administer a formalized MSE to children, but observations and parental statements are important. Many clinicians do not ever formally conduct a MSE, but their clinical observations and notations serve the same purpose.

Whether conducted formally or informally, the MSE evaluates items such as the client's appearance, posture, speech, and judgment. It is not a separate portion of the diagnostic interview but is administered throughout the intake session. Nevertheless, mental status observations are generally documented in a separate section of the psychological report.

Without conducting an MSE, there is an increased risk of misdiagnosis, especially for clients with poor insight, thought disorders, or who are in denial. For example, a client might deny being upset or agitated, but the clinician may observe several such behaviors during assessment. Simply considering the client's responses to questions the therapist has posed will not help the therapist reach a diagnosis in such cases. The observations and clinical interpretive skills employed in the MSE will aid in differential diagnosis and will provide the therapist with cues regarding how to proceed with the intake.

As noted, MSEs are available in a variety of formats, but most provide similar content. Frequently, the information gathered in the MSE is presented as a checklist of items the clinician observes and notes in the assessment. The areas most commonly reported in an MSE include:

- Appearance.
- Activity level.
- Speech/Language.
- Attitude.
- Affect/Mood.
- Stream of consciousness.
- Thought content.
- Hallucinations.
- Sensorium/Cognition.

APPEARANCE

Descriptors of appearance should be objective and include aspects such as the client's neatness and cleanliness of dress, grooming, hygiene, body odor, and apparent health. An unusual appearance could signify a number of concerns. For example, loud, expensive, or bright clothing is not unusual during a manic episode or may suggest a Cluster B personality disorder. The lack of, or inappropriateness of, certain clothing might represent cognitive concerns or confusion of thought. Impeccable dressing, or a client who constantly straightens an article of clothing, may indicate obsessive/compulsive concerns. Depression, substance abuse, a thought disorder, or dementia might be depicted in clothing that is noticeably soiled, wrinkled, or foul in odor. Nevertheless, a client's appearance alone should not influence the diagnosis. The client's subculture, background, socioeconomic status, and current situation must be taken into account before passing judgment. Consider a therapist's observations about a particular client:

> The client appeared at the interview wearing worn jeans and several layers of soiled clothing. He was 6 feet tall, weighed 110 lbs., and seemed to be poorly nourished. He appeared to be at least 10 to 15 years older than his chronological age of 38, as evidenced by a slumped posture, graying hair, decayed teeth, a rosy complexion, disheveled hair, and several facial wrinkles. He appeared to be in below average health. There was a strong smell of alcohol on his clothing and breath.

Always consider the context of the client's appearance. The previous narrative would be viewed in a different light if it were preceded by a statement that the client is homeless and living in an abandoned building with several alcoholics, than if the client were being evaluated for a job promotion.

As noted in the previous example, the client's posture may also indicate a variety of nonverbal attitudes, pain disorders, or levels of affect (e.g., slumped—signifying depression; leaning forward—signifying interest; erect—signifying anxiety or other concerns). Changes in the client's body position during the interview may signal pain, anxiety, or feelings of discomfort.

Other information that can be gleaned from observing a client's appearance includes a description of whether or not the client's appearance matches his or her chronological age, facial expressions, level of eye contact, or any other unusual physical characteristics that could indicate psychological or physical dysfunction. It is not necessary to list every possible observation; rather, the clinician should report only those that may be clinically significant or affect the validity of the interview.

ACTIVITY LEVEL

Activity level, body movements, and motor behaviors may reflect a wide range of psychological concerns. The clinician should report any unusual movements; otherwise, the report should indicate that the client did not exhibit abnormal body movement behaviors. Numerous clinical terms are available to describe various body movement behaviors; however, it is best to describe

TABLE 4.1

Clinical Observations and Everyday Language Definitions of Observable Body Movements

Clinical Terminology	Everyday Language
Akathisia	The client reports feeling restlessness in legs since the onset of neuroleptics.
Akinesia	Few movements in areas such as arm movement when walking and eye blinking.
Athetoid movements	Slow, involuntary, snakelike movements were observed in the client's arms.
Choreiform movements	Quick, jerky, involuntary movements were noticed in the client's limbs.
Dystonia	The client's head remained twisted for several minutes, during which time the client's tongue remained stuck out.
Hypokinesia	Very few body movements were noticed such as the client's arms rarely moved when the client walked.
Masked facies	There was no facial expression.
Psychomotor agitation	The client had difficulties sitting still and appeared restless and tense.
Psychomotor retardation	Body movements and speech patterns were slow.
Waxy flexibility	Client's body position, in which arms were extended upward, remained unchanged despite all attempts to change it by staff.

them in layman's terms for the benefit of nonclinician third-party reviewers. This makes reports more readily understandable, yet preserves clinical integrity.

Some clinicians choose to incorporate technical terms in the report and then define them. Table 4.1 demonstrates the difference between clinical terminology and everyday language. Although the same message is being portrayed, the level of understanding is more widespread using everyday language.

SPEECH/LANGUAGE

Observing a client's speech presents important diagnostic information regarding the client's mental status. Speech aphasia describes problems with grammar, word usage, and sentence structure. Unusual speech patterns may indicate affective, neurological, psychotic, physical, or cognitive dysfunctioning. Clinicians must be careful not to pass judgment based on speech patterns alone, but rather use such information as a piece of the puzzle to be integrated and concordant with other observations.

It can be difficult to differentiate between speech problems resulting from organic versus psychiatric etiology. Although symptoms tend to overlap, organic speech problems tend to be progressive, unless they follow a traumatic event such as a stroke. Psychiatric speech problems, on the other hand, tend to wax and wane concordant with psychiatric episodes. The MSE should consider a number of aspects related to a client's speech, including:

- Vocabulary.
- Volume.
- Pace.
- Details.
- Reaction time.
- Pitch.
- Articulation.
- Spontaneity.

Although no clear standards are defined, the MSE should report any departures from what is considered normal by the clinician. Because such information is based on opinion, observed examples should be provided. If no abnormal speech behaviors are evident, the therapist should note this as well. For example, the therapist might record, "The patient expressed a normal range of vocabulary, volume, reaction time, details, pace, pitch, articulation, and spontaneity," or "No speech concerns were noted."

When abnormal speech patterns do exist, further observations, such as whether or not speech is pressured, hesitant, monotonous, slurred, stuttered, cluttered, mumbled, and whether or not repetitions, neologisms, difficulties with word finding, or echolalia are present, should be reported. In such cases, the therapist should document specific examples and incorporate them into the diagnostic summary.

Language observations go beyond the specific areas of speech. Therapists should evaluate and record the client's level of comprehension throughout the interview. Therapists also should document the client's ability to understand simple to complex requests or points of conversation. For example, a therapist might document a client's unusual speech patterns and comprehension as:

> Speech was approximately 80% understandable due to poor articulation, slurring, and rapid pace. Vocabulary and details were below average. Volume was loud, especially when the client became agitated.

ATTITUDE

The client's attitude toward the examiner is important in assessing areas such as relationship to authority, social behaviors in new situations, prognosis of treatment, and accuracy of information. In addition, personality disorder variables are often reflected in the client's attitude. Assessment is possible across several dimensions that should be considered on a continuum and include aspects such as level of interest, cooperation, frankness, defiance, evasiveness, defensiveness, guardedness, manipulation, hostility, hesitance, ability as historian, and sense of humor.

In the case of a cooperative client, a statement such as, "The client was cooperative, friendly, provided adequate historical information, and did not appear to be guarded or defensive," portrays a reasonable picture. When the client is not cooperative, the clinician should document abnormal behavior. For example, a clinician might note:

> The patient entered the office yelling at the receptionist, "all psychologists should be locked up." During the interview, the client refused to answer over half of the questions, stating that they are no one's business. She made little eye contact and sat facing away. At one point the client stated that she had not consumed alcohol in over six months; however, there was a strong odor of alcohol on her breath and clothing, noticed by three staff members and this therapist.

Therapists should integrate the purpose of the interview when making attitudinal observations. For behavioral disorders, clinicians should note observations relating to symptoms of the presenting problem or disorder. Some children (and adults) will behave differently in the waiting room than in the presence of the interviewer, so it is important to include observations of the client's behavior before and after the session, as well as during the interview. For example, children with Conduct Disorder may behave well during the interview but punch their parents or steal a magazine on the way out of the office. Likewise, children with ADHD may show no signs or symptoms of inattention or hyperactivity during the interview, but school records may indicate strong concerns. The *DSM-IV* (APA, 1994) states that even though few or no symptoms may be observed in the clinician's office, a disorder may still be present. In cases in which clinicians do not directly observe signs of a disorder, it is important to gather more information than usual from collaterals such as family members or teachers. Generally a provisional diagnosis and accompanying statements, such as "as per history" or "as per parent but not observed during the interview," are used (e.g., 314.01 ADHD, Provisional, as per history [parents' comments, school records, psychiatrist's report], not observed during the interview).

AFFECT AND MOOD

Although often used interchangeably, affect and mood reflect the emotional state of the client from different perspectives. *Affect* refers to the clinician's observations of the client's emotional state, whereas *mood* represents the client's endorsement of symptoms. Affect and mood are usually congruent, but in cases of denial, defensiveness, or confusion, the clinician's observations may differ from the client's statements.

Affective observations include behavioral notations of the client's temperament during the examination. The following descriptors are often used in describing various aspects of affect.

Range of Affect

The affective range is on a continuum and is depicted from flat to normal. *Flat affect* is the total lack of affective responses. *Blunted affect* is characterized as a severely reduced level of affect. *Restricted affect* is a level noticeably below normal. *Normal affect* indicates that a typical and expected amount of affect was observed.

Appropriateness of Affect

The appropriateness of affect is the correspondence or correlation between the client's thoughts and speech versus the observed level of affect. For example, it would be unusual for a client to describe the recent traumatic loss of a loved one while giggling. Although appropriateness is often inconsistent in cases such as guardedness or denial, it may also indicate psychopathology.

Intensity of Affect

Affective intensity is characterized as the strength of emotional responses. For example, a person who sobs intensely with extreme emotional expression is described as having *strong intensity,* whereas someone who expresses little affect would be described as displaying *mild intensity.*

Mobility of Affect

Mobility of affect refers to the time span between changes in emotional expression. For example, *decreased mobility* (also referred to as *constricted mobility*) could refer to someone who does not show normal and expected changes in affect as topics of conversation change. *Increased mobility* or *lability* is exhibited by abrupt changes in emotional states, such as going from laughing to crying to anger in an unusually short time period.

Other descriptors of affect include psychomotor behaviors, level of anxiety, irritability, and anger expression. For example, if a client appears to be anxious but denies such concerns, the report might state:

> The client often fidgeted with his fingers and bit his fingernails. On four occasions, he appeared perplexed and stuttered slightly. He often checked his watch, stating that he must get home before the rush hour or something bad might happen. But, when asked if he describes himself as nervous, anxious, or worried, he adamantly denied any such concerns.

Mood

Mood is assessed by asking the client how he or she feels. This information is crucial diagnostically and is essential for the rule-in/rule-out process that will be covered in Chapter 5. Scores of human moods exist; however, most clinicians assess only the ones that relate to *DSM-IV* diagnoses. That is, although moods such as joy, surprise, and elation may be prevalent, they are not symptomatic of psychopathology.

Again, only moods that relate to a client's presenting problem or the reason for referral or that are incongruous with a client's observed affect should be recorded. For example, if the patient complains of panic attacks at the intake, the therapist should determine which moods or symptoms are present that could correspond with those listed in the *DSM-IV* to help validate the diagnosis.

STREAM OF CONSCIOUSNESS

Stream of consciousness, also called *flow of thought,* is determined by observing speech patterns, which are presumed to indicate thought processes. Table 4.2 highlights relevant observations that can be made about a client's speech.

Flight of Ideas

An excessive number of ideas and rapid change in idea content denote a *flight of ideas.* For example, the content of one idea has a relationship with the next or an idea may last for less than one sentence:

> We went to the store in the van. Traveling is just great. It doesn't matter what the weather is like if you like people.

Associations

Loose associations refer to unrelated ideas that occur in the same sentence or within a few sentences. The words are coherent, but the content is not related and does not follow a logical sequence. Other types of associations (e.g., clang, derailment, tangentiality,

TABLE 4.2
Typical Speech Observations

Quality and Descriptions of Speech	Content of Speech
Vocabulary	Flight of ideas
Details	Loose associations
Articulation	Clang associations
Phraseology	Derailment
Volume	Tangential speech
Pace	Neologisms
Reaction time	Thought content
Pitch	Logical
Coherency	Cause/Effect
Repetitions	Relevance
Hesitancy	Hallucinations
Pressured	
Monotonous	
Slurred	
Mumbled	
Echolalia	
Rambling	
Word finding difficulties	
Mute	
Vocal tics	

and several others) also exist. Therapists should record specific examples in the psychological report. Other observations include excessive rambling, coherency of speech, logical speech, neologisms, cause and effect, and relevance of speech. These observations are rare and can indicate severe psychopathology.

Thought Content

Thought content refers to intrusive thoughts, unusual thoughts, destructive thoughts, or false beliefs that may preoccupy the client. Common preoccupations include obsessions, compulsions, phobias, or homicidal, suicidal, or antisocial thoughts. Thought disturbances, such as delusions of grandeur, persecution, or somatic concerns, may also be observed and recorded. Clinicians should also document ideas of reference such as thought broadcasting, bizarre ideations, and unusual content.

Hallucinations

Hallucinations may be optic, auditory, olfactory, tactile, or gustatory. Before noting such observations, the clinician should make certain that the client understands the context behind such questioning and that cultural and spiritual issues are considered. For example, if a highly religious person is asked, "Do you ever hear voices that no one else hears?" an affirmative answer does not necessarily imply a thought disorder. Instead, it could reflect a religious experience or belief.

No matter what kinds of hallucinations are reported, it is important to clearly document the degree of the disturbance. Simply stating that hallucinations exist does not present a clear clinical picture. Similar to other signs and symptoms, it is important to document the onset, frequency, duration, severity, and resulting impairments of the hallucinations. Other notations of clinical significance related to hallucinations include depersonalization, derealization, deja vu, overvalued ideas, and illusions, all of which suggest issues of perception.

SENSORIUM / COGNITION

This section of the MSE elicits information regarding the client's orientation, concentration, attention span, memory, and ability to hold a normal conversation.

Orientation × 3

This refers to the client's knowledge of the current time, place, and person. The therapist typically asks the client to state the time of day, date, year, and season; the name of the clinic and the city where the interview is taking place; and the client's name and the names of other important people in the client's life. Disorientation indicates memory dysfunction that could stem from a number of etiologies.

Attention and Concentration

Attention is the ability to focus on a given task, whereas concentration is the ability to sustain attention over a period of time. The MSE measures attention and concentration by recording the client's ability to perform various mental tasks. Examples of common attention/concentration tasks in the MSE include:

- Serial threes beginning with 1.
- Serial sevens backwards from 100.
- Mathematical calculations.
- Verbal tasks backwards.
- Repeating digits.

Serial Threes

Clients are asked to count to 40 by threes beginning with 1 (e.g., 1, 4, 7, 10). The common margin of error is 0 to 2 mistakes, with an average of 2 to 3 seconds between digits. It is important to record the number of errors as well as the time that elapses between digits, the client's level of persistence, anxiety and frustration, and any strategies the client uses to perform the calculations in the report.

Serial Sevens from 100 Backwards

This task is more difficult than serial threes. The normal margin of error is 0 to 2 mistakes, with an average of 3 to 6 seconds between digits. For this test, the client is asked to count backwards from 100 by sevens. The clinician should make similar observations as the ones suggested for serial threes.

Mathematic Calculations

Depending on the client's level of education, the clinician can present mathematical calculations that are typically beyond rote memory. For example, adult clients might be asked to solve problems such as 65/5 and 12 × 6. Much simpler problems, such as asking a first grader to add 3 + 4, are given to children.

Verbal Tasks Backwards

Most adults are able to spell words such as world and earth, forward, but during times of experiencing difficulty with concentration, errors are common when spelling words backwards. Be sure to evaluate or estimate the client's intellectual level and any learning disabilities prior to making conclusions in such tasks. It is always safe to ask the client to first spell the words forward before attempting to spell them backwards. If the client is not able to spell the word forward, choose a simpler word or select a new task. Other tasks include operations such as saying the months of the year backwards or tasks that are not a challenge when recalled forward but are not typically performed backwards.

Repeating Digits

The average adult is able to repeat 5 to 7 digits forward and 4 to 6 digits backwards. The Wechsler intelligence test manuals provide child and adult norms for digit span. To administer the test, the therapist repeats an increasing number of digits, spaced one second apart and beginning with two digits forward, to the patient. The patient then repeats the digits back to the therapist in the same order. After a limit has been reached, the patient is asked to repeat another set of digits backwards.

JUDGMENT

Judgment is assessed by asking the client direct questions about hypothetical situations in which choices of judgment must be made. Questions from the Wechsler comprehension subtests are commonly used. Clinicians should bear in mind that although many clients are aware of what should be done in a particular situation, in real life they seldom take the best course of action. In this case, obtaining an accurate history of the client's behaviors will better support the clinician's determination of the client's judgment.

It is common to ask hypothetical questions such as, "What would you do if you were the first one in a theater to see smoke and fire under one of the exit doors?" Observations include the quality of the answer and whether the answer is unusual. For example, if the client answers, "I'd yell fire," it is not an unusual response, but it may indicate lack of planning or impulsivity. An answer of, "I'd just leave," begs the question, "What about the other people?" Some clients will respond, "I would warn them as I left," whereas others would respond, "That's their problem." The query, in this case, provides valuable clinical information.

INSIGHT

A client's level of insight is important in assessing treatment prognosis. Lower levels of client insight generally indicate that the client will be less aware of psychological problems. Many therapists use more behavioral counseling methods for clients with poor insight and more cognitive methods for higher levels of insight. Levels of insight may vary from session to session or depending on the problem being addressed and include:

1. Complete denial.
2. Slight awareness.
3. Awareness, but blames others.
4. Intellectual insight, but few changes likely.
5. Emotional insight and understanding that changes can occur.

Figure 3.2 (pp. 34–40) includes a mental status checklist on which the therapist documents various mental status dimensions. Some of the information is asked directly of the client, whereas other information is observed.

The biopsychosocial assessment, MSE, and other data collected from phone screens, presession questionnaires, and so on can be reviewed and integrated to assist the clinician in validating the diagnosis and demonstrating medical necessity for treatment. Chapter 5 explains the validation process.

HIGHLIGHTS
of Chapter 4

* The MSE provides an index of the client's current mental condition. It is like a snapshot of the moment, rather than being historical in nature.

* The MSE is based on both behavioral, physical, and affective observations of the client and specific client statements.

* MSE observations may vary from one session to the next, based on current mental status.

* Several specific MSE procedures are commonly employed to provide consistency and standardization.

* Observed speech, attitude, cognition, and affective observations are major components of the MSE.

* Thought content is generally assessed by the client's speech and language.

* The client's attitude and level of insight may be indicators of prognosis in therapy.

5

Validating a Diagnosis

Among the several purposes of the diagnostic interview is the need to document the medical necessity for services and solicit information to produce an accurate and effective treatment plan. Although it is not structured to be a counseling session, the manner in which information is solicited tends to be therapeutic for the client. If the therapist has a clear understanding of the *DSM-IV* and psychopathology and shows empathy for the client's situation, the result will often aid client insight.

The *DSM-IV* (APA, 1994) states, "In the *DSM-IV,* each of the mental disorders is conceptualized as a clinically significant behavioral or psychological syndrome or pattern that occurs in an individual and that is associated with present distress (e.g., a painful symptom) or disability (i.e., impairment in one or more important areas of functioning) or with significantly increased risk of suffering death, pain, disability, or an important loss of freedom" (p. xxi). It further explains that the syndrome must not be an expected behavior or culturally sanctioned. The documentation process continuously monitors impairments and progress to justify the medical necessity of services.

Each *DSM-IV* disorder is characterized by various diagnostic criteria such as symptoms, time frames, and impairments. Many disorders list a specific number of symptoms that must be present to justify the diagnosis. The *DSM-IV* cautions that the diagnostic criteria are guidelines meant to enhance communication among clinicians. Just as the color blue is a description of a wide array of hues and not a specific color, a *DSM-IV* diagnosis suggests a general category that aids in communication between professionals, rather than an exact description. The *DSM-IV* allows for clinical judgment in making a diagnosis when the individual does not clearly meet the diagnostic criteria, but the clinician believes that the diagnosis is warranted.

The *DSM-IV* follows a common format for classifying disorders. Although some *DSM-IV* disorders contain additional headings, the basic outline for each is:

Common DSM-IV *Disorder Classification Headings*

>   Code number
>
>   Name of diagnosis
>
>   Diagnostic features
>
>   Associated features and disorders
>
>>   Associated descriptive features and mental disorders
>>
>>   Associated laboratory findings
>
>   Specific age and gender features
>
>   Prevalence
>
>   Course
>
>   Familial pattern
>
>   Differential diagnosis
>
>   Diagnostic criteria

ESSENTIAL SYMPTOMS

Essential symptoms of a diagnosis are symptoms that must be present to make a diagnosis. These symptoms are listed in the Diagnostic Features section for each *DSM-IV* diagnosis. For example, the *DSM-IV* (APA, 1994) lists the essential features of Dysthymic Disorder as, "a chronically depressed mood that occurs for most of the day more days than not for at least 2 years (children, 1 year), (Criterion A)" (p. 345). If an adult has felt depressed most of the time for only one year, the diagnosis is not Dysthymic Disorder. Also the diagnosis cannot be made if the adult has been depressed two or more years, but only sporadically. Other essential symptoms are listed, but not all are required to be present to validate the diagnosis.

Primary and Secondary Essential Symptoms

The terms *primary essential symptoms* and *secondary essential symptoms* are not found in the literature but can be used to differentiate between two discrete types of essential symptoms. Some *DSM-IV* classifications break down essential symptoms into two types. The first includes symptoms *(primary essential symptoms)* that must be present to validate a diagnosis. The *DSM-IV* lists these symptoms first under the heading "Diagnostic Features." The second type includes symptoms *(secondary essential symptoms)* of which only a certain number must be present to validate the diagnosis. The *DSM-IV* combines both types, referring to them interchangeably as *essential symptoms.* Every *DSM-IV* diagnosis features primary essential symptoms, but not all list secondary essential symptoms.

For example, to diagnose a client with Conduct Disorder, the client must exhibit only "a repetitive and persistent pattern of behavior in which the basic rights of others or major age-appropriate societal norms or rules are violated" (*DSM-IV,* APA, 1994, p. 85). Other *DSM-IV* disorders include both primary and secondary essential symptoms. In this case, the client must exhibit the primary symptom(s) but only exhibit a certain number (dictated by the *DSM-IV*) of the other essential symptoms listed (secondary essential symptoms). For example, the *DSM-IV* criteria for Oppositional Defiant Disorder (313.81) include primary essential symptoms of a recurrent pattern of negativistic, defiant, disobedient, and hostile behavior toward authority figures that persists for at least six months. In addition, during this period, four or more of the following secondary essential symptoms must be validated: "(1) often loses temper, (2) often argues with adults, (3) often actively defies or refuses to comply with adults' requests or rules, (4) often deliberately annoys people, (5) often blames others for his or her mistakes or misbehavior, (6) is often touchy or easily annoyed by others, (7) is often angry or resentful, (8) is often spiteful or vindictive" (pp. 93–94). Each of the validated symptoms must result in disturbance in behavior that causes clinically significant impairment in social, academic, or occupational functioning.

In the previous example, eight secondary essential symptoms of oppositional defiant disorder are listed, but only four or more must be present, along with the primary essential symptom, to validate a diagnosis. It is, therefore, possible that two people with the same diagnosis could have no overlap in secondary essential symptoms. Even people with the same symptoms could experience different functional impairment. Thus, it is important to ensure that a diagnosis is documented carefully so that the treatment plan can be tailored to the individual client. A treatment plan that addresses a generic Oppositional Defiant Disorder diagnosis is not individually targeted and may not successfully return the client to normal functioning.

ASSOCIATED SYMPTOMS

Associated symptoms are symptoms present in, or attributable to, a diagnosis but not essential to the diagnosis. They are often vegetative symptoms (e.g., weight loss, insomnia, and diminished libido) (Maxmen & Ward, 1995). The *DSM-IV* lists various associated symptoms for most diagnoses. These symptoms are not used to validate a diagnosis but provide useful information for planning treatment and understanding the nature of the client's issues. Associated symptoms within a given diagnosis can vary among individuals. Symptoms not specifically listed in the *DSM-IV* but that contribute to the client's functional impairments of a valid diagnosis may be added to the treatment plan.

Figure 5.1 describes the various symptoms associated with Dysthymic Disorder. According to the *DSM-IV* (APA, 1994), the first essential symptom (primary essential symptom #1) must be present, along with two or more other essential symptoms (secondary essential symptoms #2–#7) to validate a diagnosis. Several associated symptoms (#1–#6) may also be present but are not necessary to justify the diagnosis.

Associated symptoms provide more information specifically about the client's situation. In this case, if the symptom in criterion A were present along with all of the symptoms in criteria C, yet no symptoms from criteria B were evident, *DSM-IV* does not allow the diagnosis. (Note: The *DSM-IV* does allow for clinical judgment in such cases.)

To validate the diagnosis in Figure 5.1, the clinician should first document criteria A, and then document at least two of the symptoms listed in criteria B. The clinician may also document any symptoms from criteria C, although these do not need to be present to diagnose the disorder. In addition to documenting these symptoms, the clinician must elicit information regarding how these effects of Dysthymic Disorder are impairing either socially, occupationally, or in other areas of the client's life causing distress.

This book follows the *DSM-IV*'s definition of essential and associated symptoms; however, this book differentiates between

FIGURE 5.1
DSM-IV Symptoms of Dysthymic Disorder

A. *Primary Essential Symptoms*
(Necessary to validate a diagnosis)

    1. Depressed most of day, for more days than not, as indicated either by subjective account or observation by others, for at least two years; and

B. *Secondary Essential Symptoms*
Presence, while depressed, of two or more of the following in order to validate a diagnosis

    2. Poor appetite or overeating

    3. Insomnia or hypersomnia

    4. Low energy or fatigue

    5. Low self-esteem

    6. Poor concentration or difficulty making decisions

    7. Feelings of hopelessness

C. *Associated Symptoms*
(Not sufficient to validate a diagnosis)

    1. Feelings of inadequacy

    2. Generalized loss of interest or pleasure

    3. Social withdrawal

    4. Feelings of guilt or brooding about the past

    5. Subjective feelings of irritability or excessive anger

    6. Decreased activity, effectiveness, or productivity

Source: DSM-IV (1994, p. 349).

the two types of essential symptoms listed in the *DSM-IV* by calling them primary essential symptoms and secondary essential symptoms. In the example of Dysthymic Disorder Symptoms (Figure 5.1), the *DSM-IV* combines the primary and secondary essential symptoms, referring to them as essential symptoms.

Incorporating Essential and Associated Symptoms into the Interview

The diagnostic portion of the initial interview is designed to rule in and rule out clinical syndromes. Crucial information is provided for third-party reimbursement, clinical dialogue, and treatment planning. The information gathered in the initial interview drives the treatment plan; therefore, it must be clinically specific.

During the diagnostic interview, the clinician should ask specific questions to validate the symptoms and criteria of a diagnosis. This process of ruling in and ruling out often accounts for as much as 30% to 40% of the interview time. As noted previously, it is crucial to ask questions regarding the onset, frequency, duration, and severity of each symptom. The *DSM-IV* also requires that clinically significant distress or impairment resulting in social, occupational, or other important areas of functioning exist before a diagnosis may be made. Examples of these impairments should be documented to validate the medical necessity for treatment.

EXAMPLES OF INTEGRATING DIAGNOSIS, SYMPTOMS, AND IMPAIRMENTS

Example 1

Janette, age 24, has been diagnosed with Dysthymic Disorder (300.4; *diagnosis*). She describes the onset of her depression as three years ago when she moved out on her own. She feels depressed at least 75% of the time. There has never been more than a 2- to 3-week period in this time frame in which she has not felt depressed *(primary essential symptoms)*. Ongoing symptoms include poor appetite, fatigue, and feelings of hopelessness *(secondary essential symptoms)*. She further adds that she often isolates herself from others, and doesn't want to do much but sit around the house *(associated symptoms)*. She has never received another diagnosis of depression or mania, nor is her depression the result of a medical condition or substance abuse *(additional validation of diagnosis)*. Prior to impairment she rarely missed work and surpassed her job quotas most of the time. Over the past two years, she has missed increasingly more work due to fatigue and low motivation. Last week she was given a warning at work due to absenteeism and significantly decreased productivity *(occupational impairment)*. Prior to impairment, she was involved in sports teams and usually spent about two evenings per week with friends. Now she socializes about one evening per month, other than eating lunch daily with coworkers *(current functioning compared to previous functioning)*. She describes herself as "lonely" and "not very interested in other people" *(social impairment)*. She states that she "just feels numb" and doesn't care much about what happens in her future *(affective impairment)*. Although she knows she must eat, she states that she is seldom hungry and has steadily lost about 5 to 10 lbs. per year *(possible physical impairment)*.

Example 2

Richard, age 7, is diagnosed with Attention-Deficit/Hyperactivity Disorder, Predominantly Inattentive Type (314.00; *diagnosis*). He is described and observed by his parents, teacher, and school counselor as having persistent patterns of inattention significantly below what is expected for his level of development *(primary essential symptoms)*. Observations by this examiner and collateral information from his school and parents indicate examples of symptoms of difficulties paying attention to details at home and school, poor attention span, lack of follow-through with homework or household chores, inability to keep track of possessions, and distractibility and forgetfulness during daily activities *(secondary essential symptoms)*. He is reported to be prone to temper tantrums, stubbornness, and bossiness *(associated symptoms)*. His parents first noticed most of these symptoms about the age of four or five. Teachers began informing his parents of these issues in the first grade *(additional validation of diagnosis)*. Although educational testing indicates a normal range of intellectual functioning, he is academically performing significantly below grade level. He is not learning age-appropriate material and has been referred to the EBD program at school *(educational impairment)*. In school activities he is often ridiculed by his classmates for not paying attention. Subsequently, he has no friends and is often teased by his classmates, resulting in social withdrawal and low self-esteem *(social and affective impairment)*.

THE RULE-IN/RULE-OUT PROCESS

The following illustration provides insight into the logic of the rule-in/rule-out process. If a man in Europe wanted directions to 2525 Main St, in North St. Paul, MN, USA, he would ask questions in a logical progression. That is, he should not ask, "Where is

2525, or where is 2525 Main St.?" because there are likely tens of thousands of 2525 Main Streets in the world. Instead, he should ask how to reach 2525 Main Street in North St. Paul, MN in the USA. Thus, he is able to avoid going to several states or countries asking where 2525 Main Street is located. A logical progression of questions avoids redundancy.

This illustration employs deductive rather than inductive methods of questioning; that is, moving from general to specific questioning to reach a conclusion. This principle holds true for the diagnostic interview as well. If a clinician asks information based on secondary essential and associated symptoms alone, it will be difficult to make a diagnosis because many *DSM-IV* disorders have similar or related secondary and associated symptoms. For example, symptoms such as social withdrawal, low self-esteem, irritability, restlessness, fatigue, guilt, negativism, sleeping problems, weight changes, and poor concentration are clinically significant but are associated with several disorders including various types of depression, anxiety, pain disorders, and thought disorders. If the clinician only solicited information about these symptoms, it would be like asking how to find 2525 Main St. The person may never get home or end up in the wrong place because the question wasn't specific. Diagnostically, misdirection may or may not become a litigious issue, but it certainly raises ethical and treatment issues.

A more efficient means of ruling in or ruling out a specific diagnosis is to first survey the primary essential symptoms of various *DSM-IV* disorders. Interviewing clients concerning these symptoms differentiates the diagnostic categories, is time efficient, eliminates redundancy, and covers the spectrum of disorders. Figure 5.2 demonstrates a poor example of ruling in or ruling out specific disorders.

Although the dialogue in Figure 5.2 may suggest therapist empathy for the client's problem, it provides little diagnostic information. If the therapist assumes that the client's responses to the questions suggest Dysthymic Disorder, it may be accurate, but several other diagnoses have not been ruled out. For example, the symptoms endorsed in Figure 5.2 could suggest other *DSM-IV* diagnoses as well, including any depressive disorder, an adjustment disorder, various personality disorders, or fatigue.

Even a person with no clear mental health diagnosis who is undergoing normal life stressors might complain of these symptoms.

FIGURE 5.2
Poor Example of Rule-In/Rule-Out Process

T: Do you feel tired at times?

C: Yes.

T: Are there times when you just want to be left alone?

C: Yes.

T: Does your self-esteem seem to drop when you feel down?

C: You hit the nail on the head.

T: Do you feel uptight when you are under stress?

C: That's exactly it!

T: Is it harder to cope when you are under stress?

C: Yes. You seem to know exactly how I feel.

In this case, the Barnum effect (Klopfer, 1960), in which overdiagnosis is possible due to vague specification of symptoms, is clearly evident. The therapist is asking questions that a majority of people, with or without psychopathology, would endorse. The client believes that the therapist is right on target. But diagnostically there is no clear target! That is because the therapist is using an inductive rather than a deductive model of questioning.

Figure 5.3 illustrates a better approach to diagnostic questioning but still does not produce a definitive diagnosis. The clinical questions in Figure 5.3 have more direction than Figure 5.2, but the questions are posed randomly. In this case, the client acknowledged

FIGURE 5.3
Better, But Still Insufficient Example of Diagnosing a Disorder

---

T: Do you feel sad often?

C: Yes.

T: Are you often anxious?

C: Yes.

T: Do you ever have panic attacks?

C: No.

T: Have you been avoiding people lately?

C: I think so.

---

feelings of depression and anxiety, but the clinician did not determine their effects, significance, or relationship with the presenting problem. Eventually these questions will have to be repeated and more specific information requested.

A better way to solicit client information and approach a diagnosis is to use the rule-in/rule-out process. The *DSM-IV* is divided into 17 diagnostic categories. Each of the diagnostic categories contains diagnostic features unique from other categories. The rule-in/rule-out process allows the clinician to target information gathering and determine what information should be pursued and what is not as important, based on the client's reported symptoms and observable signs.

The clinician almost never needs to systematically go through all 17 (p. 78) diagnostic categories for each client. The nature of the client's presenting problem nearly always directs the focus of the interview. For example, a client who initially presents with complaints of depressed mood most likely is suffering from a mood disorder. As the interview progresses, it becomes clear if concerns in other areas not initially presented by the client also exist.

STEPS OF RULE-IN / RULE-OUT PROCESS

STEP ONE: Rule-In / Rule-Out Primary Essential Symptoms

Let's return to John Doe's intake session. The therapist asks a series of questions designed to rule in or rule out different categories of *DSM-IV* disorders. Keep in mind that the therapist already ruled out a substance abuse problem earlier in the interview.

(Review of Presenting Problem)   First, the therapist reviews the client's presenting problem.

T: You stated before that you are here because of depression.
JD: Yes, I've felt that way too many times in my life.
T: Have you ever been treated for any other mental health concerns?
JD: Just for the depression with Dr. Anderson five years ago that I told you about.
T: Are there any other concerns besides depression?
JD: I don't think so. The depression is bad enough.

(*Rule-Out Anxiety Disorders*)   The next questions rule out the possibility that the client is suffering from an anxiety disorder.

T: How about anxiety?

JD: What do you mean?

T: Do you often worry excessively, feel nervous, restless, or panicky?

JD: No, not often. Every once in a while I worry, but no more than anyone else with financial problems.

T: Do you have any history of panic attacks?

JD: What do you mean?

T: Do you ever experience symptoms such as dizziness, chest pain, difficulties breathing, or feeling out of control?

JD: Oh, maybe once or twice in my life, but not to that extent. I guess I'm not a worrier.

Next, the therapist rules out cognitive disorders such as delirium, dementia, amnesia, and so on. (Information from the MSE is also used to rule out these disorders.)

T: Do you have problems with memory or concentration, or have people made comments about this to you?

JD: No, not really, actually, my memory is pretty good.

The therapist also wants to rule out physical conditions that might produce a mental disorder.

T: You stated before that you are in pretty good health. Have you noticed any changes in your health or physical condition lately?

JD: I get tired or fatigued more easily, but it's not that bad.

T: How long have you felt more fatigued?

JD: Probably since I realized how depressing things are for me. I think it's because I used to be so active, and now I just don't feel like it. I'll get over it.

Next, the therapist rules out somatoform disorders.

T: For most of your teen or adult life have you had a history of concerns such as frequent headaches, stomach aches, nausea, diarrhea, or memory lapses?

JD: No, not more than anyone else. I've always been healthy.

The therapist also rules out schizophrenia and other psychotic disorders.

T: Have you ever, or do you ever hear voices, and no one is there?
JD: Oh no!
T: Do you ever see things that no one else sees?
JD: What do you mean?
T: Like shadows walking on the wall or images that no one else sees but you.
JD: No, nothing at all like that.
T: Do you ever experience any unusual body sensations, smells, tastes, or feelings?
JD: Not at all.

Now, the therapist rules out mania.

T: Are there times in which you feel full of energy, maybe have little or no need for sleep, and feel like you are on top of the world?
JD: I wish I felt that way . . . no, not at all.

The therapist then rules out dissociation.

T: Do you ever feel like you have left your body or do you feel like you are someone else?
JD: Not at all, what you see is what you get!
T: Have you ever had times when it felt like you just were not there, but your body was going through the motions?
JD: No, never.

Next, the therapist rules out eating disorders.

T: Do you have any concerns in any of the following areas? . . . eating, such as throwing up, or eating too much or too little?
JD: My appetite is high and I've gained weight, but I'm not throwing up or binge eating.
T: Have you had any eating problems in the past?
JD: When I get depressed I gain weight.

And the therapist rules out a sleeping disorder.

T: Do you have problems falling asleep, sleeping too much or too little?

JD: Well, since my wife died I've been waking up about an hour earlier than I'd like, but I'm getting used to it.

T: Once you fall asleep do you have any problems with terrors, nightmares, or sleepwalking?

JD: No, I don't.

Next, the therapist rules out sexual or gender-identity disorders.

T: Do you have any sexual concerns or problems with sexual behavior?

JD: I've had no sex life since my wife died, but there are no sexual problems.

The therapist also rules out impulse control disorders.

T: Are any of your behaviors difficult to control or do they get out of hand?

JD: No, this is not a problem.

T: Are there any areas of your life in which others have told you that you spend too much time or effort?

JD: What do you mean?

T: Like gambling, drugs, alcohol, sexual behaviors, or even time on the computer . . . anything like that?

JD: No, not at all.

Finally, the therapist rules out adjustment disorders.

T: Have there been any other major stressors or changes in your life in the past six months that are difficult to cope with now?

JD: None that I can think of.

These diagnostic questions were designed to rule in or rule out primary essential symptoms of most *DSM-IV* disorders. Before making a diagnosis, the therapist wanted to rule out other *DSM-IV* disorders such as anxiety, panic attacks, cognitive issues, physical concerns, somatization, thought disorders, mania, dissociation, eating disorders, sleeping problems, sexual issues, and adjustment problems.

Notice that the clinician did not ask detailed questions about John Doe's depression, other than requesting a history of the problem and eliciting John Doe's concerns about it. At this point, the clinician strongly suspects a mood disorder and has ruled out most other categories of *DSM-IV* disorders.

STEP TWO: Rule-In/Rule-Out Secondary Essential Symptoms

The clinician believes that John Doe is suffering from a mood disorder and has ruled out nonmood disorders. But more specific information is needed to make a differential diagnosis. The next step is to rule in or rule out specific mood disorders, specifically a depressive disorder. The clinician ruled out a bipolar disorder during step one. The information collected earlier in the interview, as well as knowledge of specific *DSM-IV* criteria of the various mood disorders, also will be helpful in making a diagnosis. Questions in step two focus on symptomology, onset, frequency, duration, and severity of John Doe's impairments.

T: I would like to ask you some more questions about your sadness or depression.
JD: Go ahead.

First, the therapist determines how often John Doe feels depressed. *(Frequency)*

T: How often do you feel down or depressed?
JD: I feel down about every day.
T: How often do you not feel depressed?
JD: Maybe once a week.
T: What is it like then?
JD: I feel almost normal . . . like I might get ahead someday. I go shopping and take care of the things I should have done the rest of the week.

Next, the therapist finds out how long John Doe has felt depressed. *(Onset)*

T: How long have you felt this way?
JD: All of my life. I've never really been happy. I've never really felt good about myself. I'm a failure . . . but I function. . . . That's all I do. It's just that now things are building up, and I need help. My rut is deeper than usual.

The next questions seek to verify the diagnosis of a specific disorder. *(Differential diagnosis)*

T: Have there ever been any extended periods of time when you were not depressed, say for more than two months?

JD: No, none that I can remember. Sometimes when major life events are taking place, like my graduation or getting married, I've felt better for a few weeks or so, but this is unusual.

T: Tell me more about how the depression now is different than your usual mood.

JD: Like I said before, I'm usually able to function, but now I don't want to. I'm down and don't feel like getting up. There's too much pressure. I'm alone, no one cares. I feel like I'm bottoming out. It's like . . . what's the use?

T: It sounds like you are usually down on yourself and look at life as hopeless, but now things are much worse than usual.

JD: That's exactly what I'm saying.

Now the therapist needs to determine how long this most recent bout of severe depression has lasted. *(Most recent onset or cycling of symptoms)*

T: Since you have felt depressed, has there been a time in which symptoms became noticeably worse?

JD: Yes, at first after her death I was handling it, but it has been getting much worse lately.

T: How long has it been worse like this?

JD: Probably about two months.

T: And nothing happened out of the ordinary two months ago?

JD: No, things just kept building up, and I began giving up.

T: Is the feeling similar to when you received counseling from Dr. Anderson five years ago?

JD: Yes, but even worse . . . at least I was married then.

Next, the therapist clarifies John Doe's specific symptoms. *(Clarification of symptoms)*

T: Do you ever have thoughts of suicide or dying?

JD: Sometimes I think it would be better for everyone if I wasn't around. I've even thought of ways to die.

T: Do you have a plan for suicide?

JD: Oh no. I would never commit suicide . . . I believe in God . . . I couldn't . . . wouldn't . . . do it.

T: Are you sure?

JD: Yes, for certain, but thanks for asking.

T: How is your appetite?

JD: I eat and eat and eat. It's never been so bad. Just six months ago I weighed 160 pounds, now I weigh almost 190.

T: Is there anything enjoyable in your life at this time?

JD: Yes, I do enjoy reading and watching movies—they seem to be an escape.

Now the therapist clarifies how depression is affecting John Doe. *(Clarification of impairments)*

T: Has your depression affected any other areas of your life?

JD: What do you mean?

T: For example, you mentioned that you are on probation at work due to excessive absences. When I ask, "Are there any other areas in your life which have been affected by your depression?" I mean areas such as your social life, your physical health, or your thinking.

JD: I sometimes don't pay attention to things, and people think I'm forgetful. It's probably because I just don't care.

T: Do you have these times of confusion or poor concentration only when you are depressed or at other times, also?

JD: It's only when I'm the most depressed . . . maybe once or twice a month since I've been down. It's part of the reason I'm missing so much work. I'm afraid.

T: For most of your life have you done well or had difficulty making decisions?

JD: It's always been a real chore. I change my mind because I believe my decisions are wrong. I never really make up my mind.

T: Tell me more about your social life.

JD: What social life? In the past few months I haven't returned any phone calls. Like I said before, I don't even spend time with my best friend. I've become a recluse. I haven't felt like getting out. I wouldn't even know what to say to someone if I were introduced to someone new. What would I talk about . . . my life is about as boring as it gets.

With these questions, the therapist has successfully ruled in both Major Depressive Disorder and Dysthymic Disorder. Some of the symptoms and impairments were validated in the initial screening, whereas others were validated when the therapist explored symptoms of specific mood disorders. As you can see from the *DSM-IV* description of essential symptoms (Figure 5.4), the diagnosis is valid for both disorders.

FIGURE 5.4
Diagnosing John Doe with Major Depressive Disorder and Dysthymic Disorder

Diagnosis #1   Major Depressive Disorder

Must exhibit symptom in Criteria #1 and at least four symptoms from Criteria #2.

Criteria Met (X)   *DSM-IV Essential Symptoms Criteria*

Criteria #1 (Primary Essential Symptom)

X   Usual depressed mood or lack of pleasure, continuously for two or
            more weeks, resulting in social, occupational, and affective impair-
            ment or distress.

Criteria #2 (Secondary Essential Symptoms)

X   Weight gain of over 5% per month
X   Iincreased appetite
            Insomnia or hypersomnia
            Psychomotor agitation or retardation
X   Fatigue
X   Worthlessness or guilt
X   Poor concentration
X   Thoughts of death/suicide

Diagnosis #2   Dysthymic Disorder

Must exhibit symptom in Criteria #1 and at least two symptoms from Criteria #2.

Criteria Met (X)   *DSM-IV Essential Symptoms Criteria*

Criteria #1 (Primary Essential Symptom)

X   Depressed more days than not for at least two years

Criteria #2 (Secondary Essential symptoms)

X   Poor appetite or overeating
            Insomnia or hypersomnia
X   Low energy or fatigue
X   Low self-esteem
            Poor concentration or difficulty making decisions
X   Feelings of hopelessness
            Other *DSM-IV* Criteria
X   Not symptom-free for more than two months in past two years
X   Disorder not better accounted for by other *DSM-IV* conditions

STEP THREE: Determine Associated Symptoms

The previous two diagnoses of Dysthymic Disorder and Major Depression were ruled in during the interview via steps one and two. Now sufficient information is available for the treatment plan. Additional questions posed in the interview could include eliciting additional associated symptoms to aid in providing a more clear understanding of the client's issues. Clinicians may also focus on items of interest helpful within their school of thought. For example, those from a systems approach will focus on the role of the family and significant others, whereas those from a dynamic approach will show more interest in how the client's early environment has impacted the client's current state.

LIMITATIONS OF THE DIAGNOSTIC INTERVIEW

The diagnostic interview is subject to limitations of validity and reliability. It is as valid as the *DSM-IV* is valid in its diagnostic categories; however, some *DSM-IV* diagnoses are more valid than others. For example, some disorders, such as Major Depressive Disorder, list clear symptoms that must be evident to make a valid diagnosis. To justify the diagnosis, the clinician compares the client's symptoms to the symptoms listed under the specific disorder in *DSM-IV*. Thus, this diagnosis is not likely to arouse much disagreement among professionals because its symptoms are clear cut.

Other *DSM-IV* disorders do not have such straightforward symptoms, and many disorders have overlapping symptoms with other disorders. In these cases, clinicians may disagree on a diagnosis based on seemingly minor points. Some examples of disorders that have overlapping symptoms, thereby limiting the validity of their diagnosis, include: (1) Bipolar Disorder and Borderline Personality Disorder, (2) Schizo-affective Disorder and Major Depression with Psychotic Features, and (3) Major Depression; Mild, Recurrent Type, and Dysthymic Disorder, among others.

The reliability of a diagnostic interview depends on the clinician's knowledge of psychopathology and the consistency of the examination. The clinician should always ask clients the same general set of questions when ruling in or ruling out various disorders. When different sets of questions are posed to different clients, important diagnostic questions may be forgotten to be asked; thus, misdiagnosis could occur. Thorough knowledge of psychopathology and the *DSM-IV* enables the clinician to stay on target. Memorizing specific symptoms of the major mental disorders is a crucial time-saving skill that enables the experienced clinician to quickly perform the rule-in/rule-out process.

This chapter has provided information to help formulate an accurate diagnosis. The next step to helping the client return to normal functioning is to formulate an individualized and detailed treatment plan.

HIGHLIGHTS
of Chapter 5

★ In order for a diagnosis to be validated, there must be a sufficient number of symptoms and resulting impairment to meet diagnostic criteria in the *DSM-IV*. Both symptoms and impairments should be clearly documented throughout the course of therapy until the diagnosis is no longer prevalent.

★ *DSM-IV* diagnoses are broken down into essential and associated symptoms.

★ Essential symptoms are those which must be prevalent in order to give a diagnosis.

★ Associated symptoms do not validate a diagnosis, but are often present when a diagnosis occurs.

★ Interviewing time can be more efficient when essential symptoms are determined before associated symptoms because most associated symptoms are common to several diagnoses.

★ The rule in/rule out process in diagnostic interviewing saves much time in the interview process by systematically validating the existence (or lack of) of *DSM-IV* essential and associated symptoms and the subsequent diagnosis.

★ The mere existence of symptoms does not validate mental health problems unless they are significantly impairing to the individual.

★ The diagnostic interview is limited by both its validity and reliability.

6

Treatment Planning

Why treatment planning? Accountability, clarity, communication, compensation, competency, compliance, consistency, dialogue, direction, documentation, ethics, evaluation, focus, goals, integration, measurement, objectives, planning, standardization, strengths, symptoms, validation.

Treatment plan writing in the mental health field is a relatively recent development. Prior to the 1970s, formalized treatment plans were not part of the mental health delivery system. Early treatment plans provided little information other than vague acknowledgments that psychotherapy would occur. As managed care has increased the requirements for clinical efficacy, the quality of treatment plans has improved. The advent of managed care and regulatory agencies such as JCAHO, Champus, and Medicare have led to increasingly more stringent accountability procedures; therefore, detailed treatment planning is now an important part of the therapeutic process. Currently, regulatory agencies and third-party payors have similar requirements in treatment plan writing.

A survey conducted by this author of more than 2,000 mental health professionals revealed that less than 3% of currently practicing mental health professionals (e.g., psychologists, social workers, and counselors) were formally trained or supervised in accountability procedures such as treatment plan and progress note writing. A myriad of texts have been written about mental health treatment and how to conduct therapy, but few teach how to write and follow treatment plans or document the course of therapy.

COMPUTERIZED TREATMENT PLANNING

Siegel and Fischer (1981) noted that the treatment plan is the most frequently consulted portion of a client's chart. One of the biggest complaints about writing detailed treatment plans is the time it takes to develop them. (Galasso, 1987; Ormiston, Barrett, Binder, & Molyneux, 1989; Walters, 1987). Luckily, research in computerized treatment planning has flourished, and computer-generated treatment plans have become an effective and time-saving resource to clinicians.

Some early computer programs provided "canned" treatment plans that were designed for diagnostic purposes and not for treating the client's individual needs or alleviating functional impairments or distress. Some facilities use these treatment plans with potentially disastrous results. For example, a therapist might diagnose a client with Dysthymic Disorder and then pull out a "Dysthymia Treatment Plan" from a packet of several diagnostic choices. To begin treatment, the therapist fills in the client's name and signs the pre-written plan. Although treatment plans of this variety are better than no treatment plan, they are designed to address global symptoms of a diagnosis and ignore the client's special needs and desires. These types of plans do not allow the therapist to develop a collaborative and individualized plan for treating specific clients who may have unique symptoms and impairments.

Widespread accepted standards and language in treatment plan writing are developing, however, and computer software development over the past 10 years has provided some promising solutions. Today's computerized treatment plans have added increasingly more options for the therapist to individualize treatment. The *Therascribe®* treatment planner (Wiley, 1997) has received high reviews from managed care and regulatory agencies because it allows the clinician to customize the course of treatment based on the client's needs and it follows current guidelines. It is user-friendly and saves considerable time in the writing process.

Little has been published that demonstrates *how* to write treatment plans with measurable and observable objectives that meet current managed care criteria other than the guidelines for each agency. This chapter shows how to integrate current agency and managed care requirements into properly documented, individualized treatment plans.

GETTING STARTED

Treatment plan objectives should be formulated to alleviate a client's functional impairments resulting from symptoms of a *DSM-IV* disorder. It is important that treatment plans be designed to address individual clients' impairments rather than to address global symptoms.

Writing treatment plans is easiest for clinicians who are thoroughly knowledgeable with the *DSM-IV* and competent in diagnostic interviewing techniques. Excellent texts that integrate both areas include Othmer and Othmer's *The Clinical Interview Using DSM-IV* (1994), Groth-Marnat's *Handbook of Psychological Assessment,* Third Edition (1996), and Morrison's *DSM-IV Made Easy* (1995).

TREATMENT PLAN DEVELOPMENT

An individualized treatment plan is based on a detailed and accurate clinical diagnosis that has been validated by meeting *DSM-IV* criteria for the disorder and by related interview information. Further, the treatment plan must correspond with the client's specific *DSM-IV* symptoms and respective functional impairments. Treatment plans target symptoms when formulating strategies to alleviate functional impairments. The chance of misdiagnosis and unresponsive treatment increases if essential symptoms and resulting impairments are not validated or incorporated into the treatment plan.

Historically, third-party payors focused on the Axis I diagnosis as the primary determinant for reimbursement and the number of authorized sessions. Today, nearly all third-party payors still require an Axis I mental health diagnosis before authorizing for mental health services; moreover, there is a trend to exclude reimbursement for a growing number of specific Axis I diagnoses (e.g., Conduct Disorder, NOS diagnoses, and Adjustment Disorders). It is important for therapists to familiarize themselves with the specific authorization procedures and any exceptions for receiving services of each third-party payor. There are times in which it is possible to receive authorization for services when a diagnosis is not covered, but the documentation demonstrates medical necessity of services.

Reimbursement for services is most affected by the degree of functional impairment resulting from the mental disorder. Actuarial tables and treatment handbooks, such as Roth and Fonagy's *What Works for Whom?* (1996), and Barlow's *Clinical Handbook of Psychological Disorders* (1993), provide statistics regarding the average number of visits and types of therapy indicated for various disorders; however, the diagnosis itself does not determine the level of mental health services needed. For example, it is possible for two people to be diagnosed with the same disorder but exhibit different levels of impairment. Other factors could be impacting these individuals' functioning, including history, personality, social supports, genes, and life stressors, among others. It could be that one might need therapy to return to normal functioning, whereas the other does not. One of the several purposes of the diagnostic interview is to document this information and provide appropriate treatment recommendations.

A well-thought-out treatment plan addresses the individual's strengths and limitations. It goes beyond diagnosis, symptoms, and impairments. Responding only to *DSM-IV* symptoms may be technically correct, but may not meet a client's therapeutic needs. This book described earlier how to solicit and clearly document detailed examples of a client's level of functioning and contributing factors to mental health concerns in the initial interview. Although symptoms and functional impairments are similar concepts, fundamental differences exist. Symptoms are distinct terms by which a mental or physical disorder is defined, whereas impairments are problem areas or functional limitations in life that are adversely affected by the symptoms.

The client's presenting problem, needs, and wants should be accounted for in the treatment plan. JCAHO requires that the client actively participate in designing the treatment plan. Similar to building a house from a blueprint, both the buyer (client) and architect (therapist) work together to develop a mutually satisfying product. When people build a home, most have a fairly good idea of what they want it to look like. Likewise, many people entering therapy know what they want to accomplish. Therefore, the architect (therapist) does not simply hand them a plan and say, "This is what you get." Rather, clinicians provide direction based on their training and experience and consider the strengths and limitations of the buyer's (client's) ideas. Together they will develop a realistic and workable plan for treatment and recovery.

Third-party requirements can also affect treatment plan development. For example, third parties often limit the number of sessions per year they will reimburse for a particular client. Thus, if the insurance company limits reimbursement to 12 sessions per year, and the client is unable to pay for additional sessions, the treatment plan should be written to best utilize the 12 allotted sessions and provide for closure at the end of session 12.

Situational variables should also be considered when planning treatment. For example, if a client will only commit to two months of therapy because of an impending move, the treatment plan should be realistic, given this limitation. Lofty goals will lead to an unfulfilled course of therapy.

GOALS AND OBJECTIVES

Goals are the desired outcomes of therapy, and objectives are incremental steps used to accomplish treatment plan goals. Without specific goals and objectives to provide direction, treatment may be vague and ineffective. Measurable and observable objectives allow the therapist and client to evaluate the effectiveness of interventions, client progress, level of treatment, and when termination of treatment is possible or desirable. In addition, regular evaluation of the client's progress toward goals can serve as a stimulus to increasing motivation and direction and to staying focused on treatment plan issues. Effective treatment plans answer the questions, "Why am I in therapy?" "What will we talk about and do?" "How do I know how well therapy is working?" and "How will we know when therapy should terminate?" Progress notes, which will be discussed in Chapter 7, document that the treatment plan is being followed.

A number of publications and agencies recommend guidelines for developing treatment plans. For example, the *Consolidated Standards Manual* (JCAHO, 1997a), presents standards for mental health services, including assessment, treatment planning, time frames, and discharge status (see Figure 6.1). Medicare also has guidelines for clinicians to follow when preparing treatment plans and requires plans to include both long-range and short-range goals (Medicare, 1984).

As mentioned previously, the therapist and client work together to establish treatment goals, but it is up to the client to

FIGURE 6.1
Selected JCAHO Guidelines for Planning Mental Health Treatment

TX.1	Treatment planning identifies care and services appropriate to the individual's specific needs and the severity of the condition, impairment, or disability.
TX.1.1	Appropriate therapeutic efforts may begin before a full treatment plan is formulated.
TX.1.2	A preliminary treatment plan is developed based on an initial screening and is refined in response to additional clinical information.
TX.1.3	Qualified and competent individuals plan and provide care and services specific to the individual's needs and, as appropriate to the care and services given, in a collaborative and interdisciplinary manner.
TX.1.4	The treatment plan reflects the organization's treatment philosophy.
TX.1.5	The treatment plan reflects the individual's clinical needs, condition, functional strengths, and limitations.
TX.1.5.1	Rehabilitation services address assessed needs in accordance with an individualized written plan of care developed by qualified and competent individuals.
TX.1.5.2	Justification is documented when identified needs are not addressed.
TX.1.5.3	Individuals' perceptions of their needs are documented, as are the families' perceptions when appropriate and available.
TX.1.5.4	Individuals are encouraged to participate in developing their treatment plans, and their involvement is documented.
TX.1.5.5	The treatment plan addresses the involvement of the family when indicated.
TX.1.5.6	The treatment plan includes advocacy services when indicated to enhance the natural support system, facilitate environmental modifications, or create new supports.
TX.1.6	The treatment plan contains specific goals for achieving emotional and/or physical health as well as maximum growth and adaptive capabilities.
TX.1.6.1	Treatment plan goals are based on assessments of the individual and, as appropriate, the family.
TX.1.6.2	Treatment plan goals are linked to living, learning, and work activities.
TX.1.7	The treatment plan includes specific objectives for the goals identified in the plan.
TX.1.7.1	Objectives are expressed in behavioral terms that specify measurement of progress.
TX.1.7.2	A time frame for achieving each objective is specified in the treatment plan.

FIGURE 6.1 (Continued)

TX.1.7.3	Rehabilitation plans include a description of facilitating factors and possible barriers to using rehabilitation services or reaching rehabilitation goals.
TX.1.8	The treatment plan specifies the interventions and approaches necessary to meet the individual's needs and goals.
TX.1.8.1	When the individual's identified needs include developing skills for activities of daily living, a training program is developed.
TX.1.8.2	Activity services, when provided, are incorporated into the treatment plan to provide a consistent and well-structured framework.
TX.1.8.3	The treatment plan includes specialized rehabilitation services to restore or maintain the functional abilities of individuals with physical, cognitive, social, leisure, or sensoriperceptual impairments, or whose primary problem is mental illness.
TX.1.8.4	When individuals need services not offered by the organization, appropriate referrals are made and documented in the clinical record.
TX.1.9	The treatment plan specifies the frequency of treatment procedures.
TX.1.10	Goals are periodically evaluated and, when necessary, revised based on reassessment of the individual's current clinical problems, needs, and response to treatment.
TX.1.11	The treatment plan stipulates specific criteria for discharge or terminating treatment.

attain behavioral objectives. Therapeutic interventions, treatments, or strategies are not goals; rather they are the therapeutic means by which the goals and objectives will be achieved. Part of the intake process should include discussing what changes the client would like to make and how they might be accomplished. Some treatment strategies designed to accomplish the client's goals are implemented in the session and others are implemented outside the session (e.g., homework or referrals).

In most cases, goals should reflect the alleviation of symptoms in a positive manner. That is, they should demonstrate the desired attainment of an adaptive behavior rather than simply the alleviation of negative behaviors. JCAHO requires that treatment plan goals be linked to living, learning, and work activities. In addition, objectives should be written in observable, measurable terms so that outcomes can be evaluated impartially. For example, the goal, "increase positive social interactions," might be achieved through specific objectives (attained by the client) such as "attend one social function per week" or "attend weekly social skills group meeting." Treatment strategies might include therapist interventions such as "positive reinforcement of target behaviors" or "role playing means of meeting new people."

Treatment plans are revised as the client progresses in meeting objectives. JCAHO standards indicate that treatment goals should be periodically evaluated and revised. JCAHO does not impose a specific time frame for periodic evaluation; however, managed care companies often require treatment plan revisions after a set number of sessions or a given time period, such as every 3 months, every 6 to 10 sessions, or whenever best suits the client's needs.

A key factor to ensuring the client's successful accomplishment of objectives is how they are written. When objectives are either too simple or too difficult, clients will not be appropriately motivated to accomplish them. For example, extremely low expectations or easy objectives provide the client with little motivation to change behavior. Overly high expectations, on the other hand, can produce anxiety, resulting in the client's avoidance of the objective targets.

Likewise, vague and unclear objectives may lead to lengthy treatment but provide little or no direction regarding how they will help the client reach treatment goals, thereby reducing the probability of behavioral change. The obvious problem of establishing vague objectives such as "increase social interactions" is the difficulty in demonstrating significant change. For example, because the word "increase" is not quantified, even change of .001% implies attainment of the objective. Change of this magnitude will most likely not significantly change the client's level of impairment. Specific objectives clarify progress in treatment. Thus, clearly written treatment plan objectives that require a moderate amount of effort to achieve provide the greatest probability of attainment or success.

As noted, treatment plans are not static. As objectives are accomplished, they are revised to more closely attain the stated goal. If each objective is a step toward the goal, then the last objective best reflects the goal (Goodman, Brown, & Dietz, 1992). This does not mean that every change in a treatment plan requires a new form to be filled out. Incremental revisions may be noted in case notes, and the treatment plan only revised as necessary (e.g., as required by third parties or institutional policies or when writing a prior authorization request). Treatment plans

FIGURE 6.2
Revising Objectives to Reach Targeted Goals: Increase Social Interactions

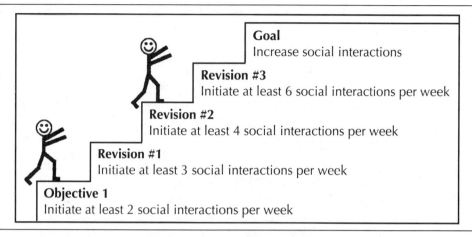

Goal
Increase social interactions

Revision #3
Initiate at least 6 social interactions per week

Revision #2
Initiate at least 4 social interactions per week

Revision #1
Initiate at least 3 social interactions per week

Objective 1
Initiate at least 2 social interactions per week

extend for a specified period or number of sessions after which they are to be revised to reflect therapeutic progress.

The timing of treatment and the number of steps needed to accomplish treatment goals are highly related to the client's degree of impairment. Figure 6.2 depicts the relationship between goals and objectives by illustrating how incrementally more challenging objectives will help a client reach a target number of initiated social interactions. Figure 6.3 features objectives that demonstrate

FIGURE 6.3
Revising Objectives to Reach Targeted Goal: Systematic Desensitization to Airplane Travel

Fly in a plane!

Fly in a plane independently
Fly in a plane with therapist
Board a plane with expert
Trip to airport with therapist
Imagine self boarding airplane
Imagine self preparing for trip to airport
Watch a movie about aircraft
Read about how planes fly
Discuss rational/irrational beliefs about flying
Vent feelings about fears of flying in airplane

incremental steps toward a goal of systematic desensitization to airline travel. Although a treatment plan would not be rewritten every time an objective is reached, the progress notes could document revisions to it.

Figures 6.2 and 6.3 illustrate how incremental objectives are used to help clients attain a goal. If, for example, the client in Figure 6.3 was initially given the objective of flying in a plane, it might be overwhelming. Incremental objectives allow the client to gradually make therapeutic progress.

Other variables, such as the client's motivation, insight, and cooperation and rapport with the therapist, as well as the therapist's clinical skills, must be considered in the timing of treatment plan objectives. In many managed care settings in which the number of sessions is limited, time becomes a precious commodity. Clinicians unused to working under time limitations sometimes view this as a deterrent to progress.

Cognitive dissonance can occur when the therapist's training and current mandates are in conflict and often results in stress, discomfort, complaining, and worrying. The dissonance can be reduced when specific training and experience in current documentation and time-limited therapeutic procedures are provided. The dissonance often stems from the stress induced from lack of training; therefore, additional training will help change the therapist's attitude and behaviors.

TREATMENT PLAN REQUIREMENTS OF THIRD-PARTY PAYORS

Third-party payors, such as insurance companies and managed care providers, have their own rules and regulations regarding development and maintenance of treatment plans. Figure 6.4 depicts common requirements.

BEHAVIORAL OBJECTIVES: MEASURABLE AND OBSERVABLE

Terms such as measurable and observable, as required by managed care companies and regulating agencies, follow the scientific practitioner model, in which empirical or observable evidence is crucial to outcomes. Vague treatment plans, for example, might

FIGURE 6.4
Third Party Payor Requirements for Treatment Plan Development and Maintenance

Competence: The service provider must have appropriate credentials to perform the indicated type of service and must be competent in the area of expertise for the particular mental disorder.

Medical Necessity: There must be documentation of dysfunction or functional impairment resulting from a mental disorder (defined in DSM or ISCD) that significantly interferes with the client's activities of daily living.

Goals/Objectives: The treatment plan must include specific, attainable, observable, and measurable goals and objectives.

Treatment: Level and amount of treatment must be concordant with intensity of impairment. Type of treatment must be consistent with acceptable procedures that reliably predict outcomes. Treatment is directed toward the active signs of a disorder.

Ongoing Documentation: Progress notes must follow specific treatment plan objectives designed to alleviate functional impairments that have been clearly documented in the assessment and in the treatment plan.

include the objective: increase communication skills. In this case the concept of communication skills is not clear. The term communicate might be interpreted as anything from a client's poor speech patterns to his or her ability to express emotions. Specificity is needed. In addition, because the objective is stated in relative terms, measurement is not possible. As noted earlier, objectives incorporating words such as increase, decrease, add, change, and so on, with no further clarification, are vague because they do not quantify the degree of change.

Measurable and observable behaviors are developed from a client's functional impairments resulting from a diagnosed mental health disorder. It is suggested that the clinician determine the symptoms of the disorder and question the client about functional impairments in the initial interview. The clinician should then determine baseline measures for the functional impairments and set goals and objectives for treatment.

It is difficult to measure and observe symptoms, but the resulting impairments are easily documented in a measurable manner. For example, documenting that a client is 75% depressed is a poor attempt to provide measurable evidence of impairment because the construct of depression is too vague to quantify. But the behavioral effects of depression can be quantified. For example, "The client misses school 75% of the time due to depression."

Subjective Units of Distress (SUD)

Symptomology can be measured using Subjective Units of Distress (SUD), which are measured on a scale of 1 to 100. Clients periodically are asked to rate their level of distress for variables such as anxiety, fear, depression, and so on. Clinicians who utilize this technique will ask clients to rate their SUD levels at the onset of therapy and then ask them to periodically reassess those levels as therapy progresses to evaluate the effects of treatment. The treatment plan can incorporate goals and objectives based on a client's SUD levels. For example, the treatment plan might state:

> Anxiety level when leaving the house. Current SUD: 90. Goal: 30. Four-week objective: 70.

Figure 6.5 illustrates a client's SUD using a graph.

VARYING BELIEFS AND PROCEDURES

Some therapeutic schools of thought claim that incorporating measurable outcomes contradicts their basic tenet of therapy. This statement might be true if measurable outcomes focused on symptoms rather than impairments. For example, many insight-oriented

FIGURE 6.5
Graphic Representation of Subjective Units of Distress (SUD)

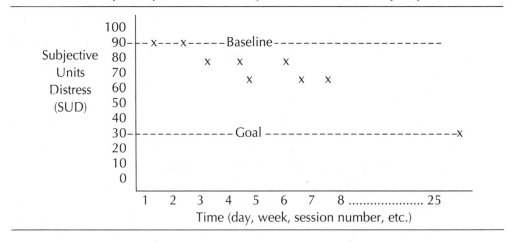

clinicians do not view therapeutic progress in terms of reducing symptoms. They believe that "symptom substitution" will occur, that is, new symptoms emerge as others decline. They do not focus on symptoms because they believe that the underlying causes of the symptoms should be the focus of therapy. Therefore, a systematic measurement of symptoms becomes moot. Thus, advocates from a number of treatment modalities ask, "If we must validate a diagnosis with symptoms but do not believe that outcomes should be measured based on symptom changes, what else is there to measure?" To answer this question, it is necessary to point out that at least three processes take place in therapy, regardless of the clinician's therapeutic orientation:

1. Assessment.
2. Treatment.
3. Discharge.

Assessment

The assessment phase always includes determining whether the client needs mental health services. That is, the clinician ascertains by some means that problems exist. A major point of the assessment is to validate the diagnosis of a disorder via symptoms and resulting impairments (thereby ensuring third-party reimbursement). No matter what theoretical orientation the therapist supports, certain criteria within the mode of therapy are used to determine whether a client requires services. The measures used to determine that services are needed can also be used to determine when services are no longer necessary.

Treatment

The treatment phase varies depending on which mode of therapy is used. Whether the clinician focuses on the effects of each symptom of the original diagnosis is not the point of documentation. Instead, the clinician should document changes in impairments resulting from the diagnosed mental health disorder. Whether the clinician chooses to modify behaviors intended to reduce symptoms or focus on childhood dynamics, for example, does not matter. What matters is documenting that the treatment is alleviating the impairments that made treatment necessary.

Discharge

Treatment lasts until the client is able to adequately function in those areas that were previously impaired. Documentation is provided by regularly evaluating progress toward the goals of the treatment plan.

VALIDATING CHANGE

Validating changes in impairments is an easy documentation task compared to quantifying symptoms. The process of documenting a client's impairments is free from differences in therapeutic schools of thought because it is simply part of documenting a client's presenting problem and goals. During therapy, changes in these impairments can be achieved and measured by the objectives set. For example, the vague objective to "increase social interactions" could be revised to "initiate an average of two new social interactions per week by August 10th." When the client accomplishes this objective, it could be revised again to "initiate three social interactions per week by October 15th." Thus, the objective remains concrete and targeted, and the effectiveness of treatment is easily measured. How these objectives are achieved is not important from a documentation standpoint. For example, some therapists might use session time to teach the client to be more socially outgoing, whereas others might focus on the client's thought patterns. Still others may explore how the client's early life experiences influence his or her ability to interact with others. The treatment plan simply provides examples of behaviors for which changes will be documented to validate therapeutic progress.

The point of documentation is to show that the treatment is working. Clinicians should be careful to select objectives that are consistent with their treatment methods. The probability of success is increased when the client is instrumental in formulating the objective.

Precautions must be taken against over-measuring goals and objectives. Not all behaviors are measurable in clearly quantifiable terms; however, it is advisable to do so whenever possible. For example, it is difficult to quantify behaviors such as level of insight, respect for authority, level of self-esteem, mental confusion, and ability to concentrate.

INSIGHT-ORIENTED THERAPY AND TREATMENT PLANNING

Perhaps the most resistance to incorporating observable and measurable outcomes in treatment plans comes from therapists who conduct insight-oriented therapy. Documenting level of insight is not clearly subject to quantification, plus the concept of symptoms reduction does not fit into the theoretical frame of reference. These clinicians find the medical model frame of reference incompatible with treating intrapsychic conflicts. Nevertheless, Gabbard (1990) notes that treatment plans are an integral part of the mental health service system just as psychodynamic theory is a major part of psychiatry; therefore, the two must be integrated.

Allen, Buskirk, and Sebastian (1992) discuss and provide examples of treatment plans developed at the Menninger Clinic, in which therapists provide traditional psychodynamic treatment but document client progress in behavioral terms. Figure 6.6 represents typical psychodynamic target areas that can be documented in the listed behavioral terms. Figure 6.7 provides examples of treatment plan statements suggesting psychodynamic terminology and methods. The authors provide eight problem domains of focus in Figure 6.6 and examples of problem areas suitable for team focus in Figure 6.7.

TYPES OF MEASUREMENT

There are four traditional types of data that can be measured: nominal, ordinal, interval, and ratio. Behavioral objectives can incorporate nominal, ordinal, or interval data. There is no use for ratio data (requiring an absolute zero, which is not a behavioral concept); interval is the highest measure available in behavioral

FIGURE 6.6
Psychodynamic Target Areas in Treatment Plan Writing

Self-concept and identity

Low self-esteem/self confidence

Unclear/unstable identity/sense of self

Uncertain masculine/feminine identity

Self-concept and identity disrupted by dissociation

Interpersonal relationships

Excessive interpersonal isolation

Unstable relationships

Hypersensitivity to rejection and perceived abandonment

Inability to function autonomously

Excessive dependency

Continual perception of victimization/abuse/exploitation

Extreme distrust of others

Extreme hostility in interactions with others

Oppositionalism/indirect opposition to demands

Dishonest behavior

Extreme self-centeredness/arrogance

Hypersensitivity to criticism

Deficient social skills

Thinking and cognition

Impaired contact with reality

Disorganized thinking

Failure of accommodation to cognitive deficits

Flashbacks with confusion of past and present

Emotional functioning

Depressed mood

Suicidal intentions/preoccupation

Mood-related withdrawal from people/activities

Hyperactivity/euphoria

Tension/fearfulness/panic

Excessive and unrealistic guilt feelings

Mood swings

FIGURE 6.6 (Continued)

Impulse regulation/addiction

    Impulsivity

    Substance abuse (specify)

    Self-injurious behavior

    Violence

    Flight/elopement

    Inhibition/overcontrol

Adaptive skills

    Impairment in activities of daily living

    Impairment in academic/vocational skills

    Poor medication compliance

Family

    Lack of age-appropriate autonomy

    Alienation from family

    Marital difficulties

    Parenting problems

    Poor family alliance with treatment team

Other (including medical)

Source: J. G. Allen, J. R. Buskirk, and L. M. Sebastian. (1992). "A psychodynamic approach to the Master Treatment Plan." *Bulletin of the Menninger Clinic, 56,* 487–510.

data. Nominal data in treatment objectives demonstrate whether or not a behavior takes place. Ordinal data suggest increases or decreases in behaviors but do not quantify the amount of behavioral change. Interval data allow the observer to determine the amount of behavioral change; thus, these data are more precise than ordinal data. Table 6.1 illustrates the various means by which objectives may be measured.

TREATMENT STRATEGIES

Treatment strategies incorporated in the treatment plan should reflect acceptable (nonexperimental) interventions that have been

FIGURE 6.7
Example of Psychodynamic Treatment Plan

Example #1

Problem focus
Severe dissociation and discontinuity in identify associated with profoundly impaired interpersonal and vocational functioning. Manifested by amnesia, loss of job, propensity to be exploited by others, and inability to take care of basic needs.

Long-range goal
Patient will establish and maintain continuous self-awareness and develop a coherent sense of self.

Short-term goals (objectives)

1. Patient will report discontinuities in experience (amnesia) to self.
2. Patient will make a list of alter personalities and describe each.
3. Patient will initiate communication among alter selves.
4. Patient will identify alter personalities for staff.
5. Patient will keep a journal to record experience of alter personalities.
6. Patient will verbalized awareness of situations/feelings that trigger emergence of alter personalities.
7. Patient will take responsibility for actions.
8. Patient will verbalize understanding of the origins of his/her alter personalities/fugue states.

Example #2

Problem focus
Impaired contact with reality and extreme social isolation. Manifested by paranoid delusions, auditory hallucinations, inability to leave the house and to function at work, and deterioration of personal hygiene.

Long-range goal (a)
Patient's perception will be accurate.

Short-term goals (objectives)

1. Patient will take medication as prescribed and report effects.
2. Patient will plan and carry through a schedule of activities.
3. Patient will check out perceptions and assigned nursing/activity therapy staff.

Long-range goal (b)

Short-term goals (objectives)

1. Patient will compare beliefs with those of other patients.
2. Patient will discuss unrealistic beliefs and the psychological basis.

Source: J. G. Allen, J. R. Buskirk, and L. M. Sebastian. (1992). "A psychodynamic approach to the Master Treatment Plan." *Bulletin of the Menninger Clinic, 56,* 487–510.

TABLE 6.1
Methods for Measuring Behavioral Objectives

Type of Measurement	Definition of Objective	Sample Statement of Objective	Use
Time frames (Nominal data)	Objectives are identified by time periods in which behaviors will be evidenced/ decreased.	Client will remain sober for at least 30 days. Target date: July 9.	Easy to document by collaterals. Time is quantified, not the behavior.
Specific completion of assignments or tasks (Nominal data)	Documenting for med. evaluation, therapeutic contracts, homework, etc.	Client will visit psychiatrist by Dec. 12 for med. eval.	Documents assignments given and additional services needed.
Specific outcomes (Nominal data)	Denoting whether or not behaviors have occurred.	Client will make no suicide attempts in next 60 days. Target date: February 12.	Generally objectives are rated by others. Used in day care or in residential settings.
Increase in frequency (Ordinal data)	Increases in positive behaviors	By May 8 the client will discuss in each group on average three incidents when he has not acted impulsively after getting his way.	Use when the goal is to increase frequency of behaviors.
Decrease in frequency (Ordinal data)	Decreases in negative target behaviors	The client will decrease suicidal threats to no more than 1/week by Dec. 12.	Use when the goal is to eliminate or decrease frequency of behaviors.
Baseline Comparisons (Interval data)	Comparing levels of behaviors to a baseline measure	Client will increase positive statements to family. Current (baseline): 1/week Objective: 4/week by June 3.	Denoted in casenotes or graphs. Client easily visualizes progress as objectives are incrementally increased.

Note: Material adapted in collaboration with Steve Friedman, MA.

proven efficacious in the field. Clinicians should avoid including vague treatment strategies, such as individual therapy, because they do not adequately describe what interventions are taking place. Information in the treatment plan about specific interventions should include: (1) type of therapy (e.g., individual, group, or family), (2) school of thought (e.g., psychoanalytic, rational-emotive, or cognitive-behavioral), (3) therapeutic techniques (e.g., role playing, dream interpretation, or positive regard), (4) homework assignments, and (5) any other interventions taking place inside or outside of the session.

TREATMENT PLAN FORMATS

Treatment plan formats vary, but at minimum, headings for Symptoms, Goals/Objectives, and Treatment Strategies (or similar nomenclature) should be used. Some therapists include a separate column to list a time frame for attaining each objective. Others incorporate the same time period (e.g., 8 weeks, a particular date, or number of sessions) for the entire treatment plan, rather than setting separate time frames for reducing impairments. Some treatment plans include a column that lists specific services and providers to comply with JCAHO standards. Master treatment plans, such as those used in multidisciplinary settings, note which provider in the facility (and his or her area of specialty) will provide specific services and how often the services will be performed. When only one therapist provides services, as in private practice, no such notation is needed.

This text adopts the treatment plan format outlined in *The Complete Psychotherapy Treatment Planner* (Jongsma & Peterson, 1995) (Figure 6.8). This format complies with most third-party standards in which problem areas, goal, objectives, interventions, and diagnosis are listed. Examples of the computerized version of *Therascribe®* (Wiley, 1997) treatment plan format are included at the end of this chapter and in Appendix A.

COMMON PROBLEMS IN TREATMENT PLAN WRITING

Treatment plan writing is vulnerable to several shortcomings. The combination of complying with several regulatory agency and

FIGURE 6.8
Treatment Plan Example

Problem: RELAPSE-PRONE

Definitions: Patient has a history of multiple treatment attempts and relapse.
Friends or family members are substance abusers.
Patient has never worked on a program of recovery long enough to maintain abstinence.

Goals: Reduce the risk of relapse and maintain a program of recovery free of substance abuse.
Develop a new peer group supportive of recovery.
Develop coping skills to use when experiencing high-risk situations and/or craving.

Objectives	**Interventions**
1. Write a detailed chemical-use history describing treatment attempts and the specific situations surrounding relapse (2/12/98).	1. Have the patient write a chemical-use history describing his/her attempts at recovery. Teach the patient the high risk situations (e.g., negative emotions, social pressure, interpersonal conflict, positive emotions, testing personal control) that lead to relapse. RP: Molly Evans, M.A. Substance Abuse Counselor
2. Verbalize an acceptance of powerlessness over alcohol/drugs (2/15/98).	2. Using an AA step one exercise, help the patient see the powerlessness and unmanageability that result from substance abuse and relapse. RP: Molly Evans, M.A. Substance Abuse Counselor
3. Visit physician to see if pharmacological intervention is warranted, and take all medication as directed (2/24/98).	3. Physician will examine the patient, order medications as indicated, titrate medications, and monitor for side effects. RP: Dwight Kessler, M.D. Psychiatrist
4. List five reasons for patient's failure to work on a daily program of recovery (2/18/98).	4. Using a relapse history, help the patient understand the reasons he/she failed to work on a program of recovery. RP: Molly Evans, M.A. Substance Abuse Counselor

(continued)

FIGURE 6.8 (Continued)

Objectives	Interventions
5. Write a plan to increase reinforcement when attending recovery group meetings (2/20/98).	5. Help the patient develop a plan that will increase the rewards obtained at recovery groups (e.g., concentrate on helping others, go for dessert after the meeting, socialize, stick with the winners). RP: John Smith, Psy.D. Group Therapy Leader
6. Develop a written plan to deal with each high-risk situation (e.g., negative emotions, social pressure, interpersonal conflict, positive emotions, testing personal control) (2/22/98).	6. Help the patient develop a written continuing care plan that includes the essential elements necessary for him/her to maintain abstinence and continue recovery. RP: Molly Evans, M.A. Substance Abuse Counselor
7. Practice alcohol/drug refusal skills (2/22/98).	7. Use modeling, role playing, and behavior rehearsal to teach the patient how to say no to alcohol/drugs; then practice refusal in several high-risk situation. RP: Molly Evans, M.A. Substance Abuse Counselor
8. Make a card of emergency phone numbers to call for help in a high-risk situation (2/25/98).	8. Help the patient make an emergency card to carry at all times that has the phone numbers of people to call in high-risk situations. RP: Molly Evans, M.A. Substance Abuse Counselor
9. Develop a written personal recovery plan (e.g., be honest, regularly attend recovery group meetings, get a sponsor, and seek any other treatment needed to maintain abstinence) (2/25/98).	9. Help the patient decide on the aftercare placement that is structured enough to help him/her maintain abstinence (e.g., halfway house, group home, outpatient treatment, day care, partial hospitalization). RP: Molly Evans, M.A. Substance Abuse Counselor

Diagnosis: 303.90 Alcohol Dependence

third-party payor requirements and incorporating them into a brief document, along with a lack of training regarding how to integrate diagnosis and treatment strategies, can result in poorly documented treatment plans. Problems begin when the clinical assessment is unclear. Vague assessment procedures contribute to vague treatment plans, which lead to unfocused treatment. Other factors, such as developing nonmeasurable objectives and undefined treatment strategies, also lead to unsuccessful treatment.

Problems also arise when the treatment plan does not correspond with the *DSM-IV* diagnosis. Therapeutic interventions should not only be concordant with acceptable procedures in the mental health profession; they should also be of proven effectiveness for the specific problems being treated. Generic treatment for all clients is inappropriate treatment.

Likewise, the number of goals and objectives should be consistent with the level of care and number of sessions allowed. Setting too many goals may overwhelm the client, and there may not be enough time to adequately address each goal in the allotted number of sessions. In addition, focusing too much on outcome measures may lead to treating symptoms rather than treating the client. On the other hand, under-focusing on outcomes promotes lack of therapeutic direction. Some common problems with treatment plans include:

- Vagueness.
- Not indicative of the assessment.
- Not reflecting the diagnosis.
- Unrealistic (over/under ambitious).
- Not assessable.

TREATMENT PLAN WRITING

The content of the treatment plan is based on information obtained in the diagnostic interview, psychological testing, collateral reports, observations, and previous treatment records. The treatment plan summarizes and prioritizes this information. Jongsma and Peterson (1995) suggest following these steps in developing the treatment plan.

STEP 1: Problem Selection

Problem selection involves deciding which problem areas will be the focus of therapy. Although several problems may exist, they should be prioritized so that services will most effectively help the client. Problem areas should be expressed in behavioral terms. Remember that the treatment plan should list only problems that most effectively validate the diagnosis and show evidence of impairments.

STEP 2: Problem Definition

The problems in Step 1 should be defined according to the client's particular issues. Rather than resorting to generic definitions, problems should align with symptoms of a specific *DSM-IV* or ISCD disorder and thereby correspond with a specific diagnosis. This specificity ensures that guidelines, such as JCAHOs, are followed, and treatment is concordant with the diagnosis. Remember that problem areas should reflect areas of impairment in the client's life for which services are being sought. To ensure appropriate communication among mental health professionals, problems should be defined according to *DSM-IV* terminology.

STEP 3: Goal Development

Goals are broad descriptions of the desired outcome for each problem area. They specify behavior changes that the client must attain to demonstrate that treatment is working. Therapeutic techniques or strategies are used to reach goals but do not represent attainment of those goals. For example, the statement, "read two books about codependence," is not a goal because it does not suggest a behavior change; rather, it is a treatment strategy.

STEP 4: Objective Construction

Objectives are incremental steps to attaining goals. They must be observable and measurable to meet the requirements of third-party reviewers. They directly correspond to the impairments (e.g., social, occupational, affective, physical) by which the diagnosis was validated. Generally, each goal should have at least two written objectives. Each objective should include a target date for attainment, at which time progress is evaluated and objectives are revised to more appropriately meet the underlying goals.

STEP 5: Intervention Creation

Interventions represent the treatment strategies conducted or guided by the therapist. Interventions should be empirically valid and not contraindicated or experimental. Each objective should have at least one intervention. Documentation of therapeutic interventions should include the type of therapy (e.g., individual, group, collateral, family), treatment modality (e.g., psychodynamic, cognitive-behavioral, humanistic), and specific interventions common to the school of thought (e.g., role playing, dream interpretation, or bibliotherapy).

STEP 6: Diagnosis Determination

The symptoms included in the treatment plan must be concordant with a *DSM-IV* diagnosis. Few, if any, insurance companies will reimburse treatment without an Axis I diagnosis. Note: This author suggests that the diagnosis be determined prior to writing the treatment plan; however, Step Six is included to ensure that the treatment plan targets the client's diagnosis.

A computerized treatment plan for John Doe using the *Therascribe®* (Wiley, 1997) program appears on pp. 122–125.

SAVING TIME IN WRITING TREATMENT PLANS

JCAHO recommends that the client take an active part in establishing treatment plan goals and objectives. Some clinicians take time between sessions to write their treatment plans. A potential problem with this procedure is that it may leave out the client's participation in the process. After the initial assessment, the

FIGURE 6.9
Computerized Treatment Plan for John Doe

Treatment Plan
for
John M. Doe
by
Sigmund Z. Adler, PhD

Patient Data

Admission Date: 5/10/98	**Birthdate:** 4/6/62	
Treatment Setting:	**Age:** 35	**Init. Sessions Authorized:** 0
Patient ID: 123456	**Gender:** Male	**Add'l. Sessions Authorized:** 0
Last Review Date: None	**SSN:** 987-06-5043	**Total Sessions Authorized:** 0
On Medication?: No	**Race:** African American	**Authorized Sessions Left:** 0
Previous Treatment: No	**Status:** Widowed	**Gatekeeper:** None

Patient Strengths: Intelligent, Reasonable Judgment, Expressive/Articulate, Physically Healthy, Integrated Moral Values

Assessments Completed: Beck Depression Inventory® (BDI), Psychosocial History, Clinical Interview

Insurance Carriers:

Presenting Problems

Primary Problem: Depression

Secondary Problem(s):   Family Conflict
Vocational Stress

Other Problem(s):

Mental Status Description

Thought Disorder: No	**Dress:** Appropriate	**Long-Term Memory:** Intact
Delusions/Hallucinations: No	**Judgment:** Intact	**Short-Term Memory:** Intact
Intelligence: Average	**Mood:** Dysphoric	
Suicide Risk: Slight	**Violence Risk:** None	**Child Abuse Risk:** None
Mental Status Summary:		

Diagnosis (DSM-IV)

Axis I: 300.4   Dysthymic Disorder
296.31   Major Depressive Disorder, Recurrent, Mild
Axis II: V71.09   No Diagnosis
Axis III: Defer to Physician
Axis IV: Occupational Problems
Economic Stress
Relationship Conflicts
Axis V: **Current Functioning:**   61–70
Last Year Functioning: 81–90

FIGURE 6.9 (Continued)

Treatment Plan

A. Primary Problem: Depression

Behavioral Definitions

- Depressed affect.
- Diminished interest in or enjoyment of activities.
- Poor concentration and indecisiveness.
- Social withdrawal.
- Low self-esteem.
- Unresolved grief issues.

Long-Term Goals

- Alleviate depressed mood and return to previous level of effective functioning.

Short-Term Objectives

- Verbally identify, if possible, the source of depressed mood.
  - *   **Plan Date:** 5/10/98   **Target Date:** 9/10/98   **Projected Sessions:** 8

- Complete MMPI, Beck Depression Inventory
  - *   **Plan Date:** 5/10/98   **Target Date:** 9/10/98   **Projected Sessions:** 4

- Engage in physical and recreational activities that reflect increased energy and interest. Current: 0   3 Month objective: 2 per week
  - *   **Plan Date:** 5/10/98   **Target Date:** 9/10/98   **Projected Sessions:** 2

- Participate in social contacts and initiate communication of needs and desires. Current: 1 per month   3 Month objective: 4 per week
  - *   **Plan Date:** 5/10/98   **Target Date:** 9/10/98   **Projected Sessions:** 8

Therapeutic Interventions

- Encourage sharing feelings of depression in order to clarify them and gain insight as to causes.
  - *   **Plan Date:** 5/10/98   **Provider:** Sigmund Z. Adler, PhD   **Projected Sessions:** 12

- Ask client to write a letter to lost loved one regarding feelings of loss, anger, guilt, and so forth, and share that letter to receive feedback.
  - *   **Plan Date:** 5/10/98   **Provider:** Sigmund Z. Adler, PhD   **Projected Sessions:** 1

- Assign participation in recreational activities.
  - *   **Plan Date:** 5/10/98   **Provider:** Sigmund Z. Adler, PhD   **Projected Sessions:** 1

- Arrange administration of MMPI and/or BDI and evaluate the results.
  - *   **Plan Date:** 5/10/98   **Provider:** Sigmund Z. Adler, PhD   **Projected Sessions:** 1

- Assist in developing coping strategies (e.g., more physical exercise, less internal focus, increased social involvement, more assertiveness, greater need sharing, more anger expression) for feelings of depression.
  - *   **Plan Date:** 5/10/98   **Provider:** Sigmund Z. Adler, PhD   **Projected Sessions:** 2

- Reinforce social activities and verbalization of feelings, needs, and desires.
  - *   **Plan Date:** 5/10/98   **Provider:** Sigmund Z. Adler, PhD   **Projected Sessions:** 1

- Assess need for medication and arrange for prescription, if appropriate.
  - *   **Plan Date:** 5/10/98   **Provider:** Carl J. Erikson, MD   **Projected Sessions:** 1

(continued)

FIGURE 6.9 (Continued)

B. Secondary Problem(s)

Family Conflict

Behavioral Definitions

- A family that is not a stable source of positive influence or support since children have little or no contact with him.

Long-Term Goals

- Increase level of acceptance between client and his children.

Short-Term Objectives

- Describe the conflicts and understand the causes of the conflicts between self and children.
  * **Plan Date:** 5/10/98   **Target Date:** 9/10/98   **Projected Sessions:** 4
- Increase the number of positive family interactions by planning activities such as bowling, fishing, playing table games, doing work projects. Currently: 2 hours/week   3 Month objective: 10 hours/week
  * **Plan Date:** 5/10/98   **Target Date:** 9/10/98   **Projected Sessions:** 6

Therapeutic Interventions

- Confront client when he/she is not taking responsibility for self in family conflict.
  * **Plan Date:** 5/10/98   **Provider:** Sigmund Z. Adler, PhD   **Projected Sessions:** 5
- Conduct family therapy sessions with client and parents to facilitate healthy communication, and conflict resolution.
  * **Plan Date:** 5/10/98   **Provider:** Sigmund Z. Adler, PhD   **Projected Sessions:** 4

Vocational Stress

Behavioral Definitions

Long-Term Goals

- Increase job security as a result of more positive evaluation of performance by supervisor.

Short-Term Objectives

- Current: Absent from work 10 days/month.   3 Month objective: < 2 absences/month.
  * **Plan Date:** 5/10/98   **Target Date:** 8/10/98   **Projected Sessions:** 2

Therapeutic Interventions

- Assist client in developing a plan to be taken off probation at work.
  * **Plan Date:** 5/10/98   **Provider:** Sigmund Z. Adler, PhD   **Projected Sessions:** 1

Treatment Modalities

The following treatment modalities are being utilized:

Individual Therapy 1 time Weekly
Family Therapy   2 times Monthly

FIGURE 6.9 (Continued)

Treatment Approaches

The following treatment approaches are being implemented:

Symptom Focused Education • Solution Oriented

Prognosis

The probability of successful achievement of treatment goals is: Good.
The rationale for this probability rating is: Although there is a history of dysthymic disorder, current
concerns with depression are mainly reactive.

Criteria for Discharge from Treatment

- **Projected date for resolution of all problems:** July 19, 1998

- **Projected Total Number of Sessions Required for Completion of Treatment:** 16
  John M. Doe will successfully achieve 80% of those Short Term Objectives that have been
  marked with an asterisk before being considered for discharge from treatment.

- **Additional Criteria:**

Patient Response to Plan

Patient response to treatment plan presentation:

I, John M. Doe, have reviewed this treatment plan.

x _____   Date:_____

Provider Credentials

Primary Treatment Provider
Sigmund Z. Adler, PhD
Psychologist
License: 777-999 MO

_____   _____

Signature   Date

clinician and client can review the assessment material and co-operatively write the treatment plan during the session. This procedure increases client involvement in the treatment process and saves time. The session can be therapeutic and provide a clear understanding of the direction for therapy for clients who are able to understand the process. It is advisable to spend less time and effort writing treatment plans in session with clients with severe cognitive deficits, psychotic concerns, or those with low motivation to be in treatment.

REVISED TREATMENT PLANS

Revisions in treatment plans can be of two types: treatment plan updates or updated treatment plans. *Treatment plan updates* nar-ratively refer to the original treatment plan and describe any changes that have taken place since the original treatment plan or previous update was written. The report is similar or identical to a preauthorization for additional services report, which will be ex-plained in Chapter 8. A sample request for additional services is found on p. 172.

An *updated treatment plan* is a rewritten treatment plan re-flecting current progress. It generally includes a brief narrative of progress to date. Objectives that have been met are revised to more closely reflect goals. Those that have not been met are re-viewed to determine if other interventions could be more helpful. New objectives may also be introduced into the treatment plan at this point. A revised treatment plan, then, is similar to the origi-nal treatment plan, but it reflects the client's current state of functioning.

A properly documented treatment plan provides a solid foun-dation for documenting the course of therapy. Once the treatment plan has been developed, the next step is to put the plan into ac-tion. To keep therapy time-efficient and on track, and to qualify for reimbursement, clinicians must document that the plan is being followed and progress is being made. Progress notes serve this purpose. Progress notes are the only documentation that shows third-party reviewers whether or not treatment is working so it must be done well. Chapter 7 demonstrates how to write ef-fective progress notes that follow the treatment plan.

HIGHLIGHTS
of Chapter 6

★ Although a relatively new procedure, the treatment plan is the most frequently consulted treatment document.

★ There is a major difference between planning treatment and writing a treatment plan.

★ Because a diagnosis is based on the *DSM-IV,* the treatment plan also validates *DSM-IV* principles.

★ Treatment plans are designed to provide observable and measurable treatment outcome measures that demonstrate alleviation of functional impairments.

★ Both the client and therapist take an active part in treatment plan formulation.

★ Treatment plans are highly individualized and account for several client and therapist variables, situational concerns, and third-party regulations.

★ The client ultimately sets goals and objectives.

★ Goals reflect overall outcomes in therapy, whereas objectives are incremental, objective, and measurable steps by which goals are attained.

★ Objectives are periodically revised as treatment progresses toward the goals.

★ There are several ways to measure objectives, which allows for variations in techniques and schools of thought.

7

Progress Notes

Progress notes provide evidence that a session occurred. They are the only record for documenting the type of session conducted, length, content, interventions, and therapeutic progress. Because detailed progress notes are the primary source for documenting what happens in therapy and whether progress is being made, they are a primary tool for auditors to use when determining whether treatment is eligible for reimbursement. Clinicians must be certain, therefore, that session content is not implied but rather fully documented.

A reader should be able to determine the client's diagnosis, current issues, and effects of therapy from reading progress notes. Progress notes should correspond with the client's presenting problems and subsequent diagnosis. It is also necessary to document a client's functional impairments that have led to the medical necessity for services and the course of treatment toward alleviating those impairments. For example, if a client is diagnosed with depression, the progress notes should reflect treatment for depression and not other problems (unless they, too, have been included in the treatment plan). An auditor will review progress notes to determine whether the client's diagnosed disorder is being treated satisfactorily.

Progress notes have evolved in numerous ways in the past several years. Older styles merely documented that a session was held and informed the reader to some degree of what happened in the session. Today, progress notes are an essential documentation tool. Third-party criteria for progress notes have become increasingly more stringent in terms of accountability because, until recently, there has been little documented evidence of the effects of therapy. Third-party requirements, whether they be from regulatory agencies or third-party payors, demand behavioral evidence to demonstrate accountability for services. For financial reasons, third-party payors cannot provide unlimited mental health benefits. Regulatory agencies set high standards to raise the level of accountability and professionalism in the mental health field. Therapists must clearly document that the treatment plan is being followed and services are being directed toward the active symptoms of the diagnosis, what progress is being made, and how goals and objectives are being addressed.

Why Use Progress Notes?

In addition to third-party requirements regarding the use of progress notes, there are other benefits as well. Progress notes establish accountability to the client. Keeping therapy on track and steadily noting progress by following the treatment plan assures cost effectiveness. Progress notes are designed to provide evidence that the services being conducted are efficacious.

Progress notes are also helpful when a client is transferred to another therapist. Clear progress notes alert the new therapist regarding specific issues that have been addressed and the types of interventions that work best for the client. Progress notes also establish baseline behaviors to help evaluate progress and setbacks.

WHAT CONSTITUTES A GOOD PROGRESS NOTE

Several questions that progress notes should address are shown here:

1. What content or topics were discussed in the session?
2. How did the session address treatment plan objectives?
3. What therapeutic interventions and techniques were employed and how effective were they?
4. What clinical observations (behavioral, affective, etc.) were made?
5. What progress or setbacks occurred?

6. What signs and symptoms of the diagnosis are present or no longer present?

7. How are the treatment plan goals and objectives being met at this time?

8. What is the current medical necessity for services?

9. What is being done outside the session?

10. What are the client's current impairments and strengths?

Answering these questions documents that appropriate treatment is being provided. It is not necessary to address each question in every progress note; rather, a pattern of documentation should be established so that each question is adequately addressed over the course of therapy. Let's consider each question individually.

What Content or Topics Were Discussed in the Session?

Historically, progress notes have focused primarily on session content. Although this information is important, it does not sufficiently document medical necessity. Statements should be objective and factual and include information regarding current, ongoing, or historical events in the client's life; facts about certain diagnoses; and other topics that come up during the session.

At least one statement in each progress note should mention the session's content. If more than one topic is discussed, each topic should be listed in the order it was addressed. Topic areas should coincide with the areas of impairment addressed in the treatment plan. If topic areas do not seem to relate to the primary purpose of treatment, the purpose and medical necessity for covering the topic should be documented.

Examples of content-oriented progress note statements include:

1. "Discussed ways in which family of origin influences current behaviors."

2. "Session focused on the four times client has been in the hospital for suicidal gestures."

3. "Client asked to help explore problems coping with rejection."

How Did the Session Address Treatment Plan Objectives?

As noted, one of the main functions of progress notes is to document that treatment plan goals and objectives are being addressed. Progress notes should specify which treatment plan objectives are being treated and how they are progressing.

If, for example, a treatment plan addresses the client's depressed mood in each problem area, goal, and objective, but progress notes document that communication skills in the client's marriage are the focus of treatment, treatment plan goals and objectives are not being addressed or met. To avoid this, it is helpful to assign a number or letter to each treatment goal and objective and list in the progress notes which ones are being treated each session. It is common to denote the goal as a number and the related objectives as alphabetical characters following the number. For example:

> Goal 1: Increase self-esteem.
>
> > Objective 1a: Initiate at least 2 positive behaviors per week, as identified in Session 2.
> >
> > Objective 1b: Employ at least 3 assertive behaviors per week.

In this case, the progress note statement could read: "Worked on Objective 1b by role playing various assertive behaviors." Additional statements could indicate specific issues and interventions being employed to address treatment objectives.

What Therapeutic Interventions and Techniques Were Employed and How Effective Were They?

Progress notes include specific therapeutic interventions for a number of reasons. First, several studies indicate that some treatment strategies are more effective than others in certain circumstances. As well, some treatment strategies are experimental, and others have been demonstrated to be nonefficacious in certain therapeutic situations. It is not unusual for a third-party insurance or managed care contract to specifically state that the policy does not cover experimental therapeutic procedures.

The treatment plan lists which therapeutic school of thought and subsequent procedures will be employed in the treatment. Progress notes verify that the procedures are being used and demonstrate the outcomes of implementing the procedures. Such documentation helps the clinician evaluate the effectiveness of treatment and decide whether changes to the treatment plan should be made.

Documenting specific treatment interventions also helps the therapist keep the session on track and therapeutic. Without them, sessions could deteriorate to chit-chat or discussions irrelevant to treatment. Many short-term therapy models focus on remaining on target and being therapeutically consistent throughout treatment.

What Clinical Observations (Behavioral, Affective, etc.) Were Made?

The therapist's clinical observations are crucial in evaluating both the course of therapy and assessing the client's current condition. Notations should include clinically significant observations of verbal and nonverbal behaviors. Observations should be integrated with the client's presenting problem and diagnostic concerns. For example, if a client is diagnosed with depression, progress notes should regularly assess the client's level of depression. It is expected that the client would appear less depressed as therapy progresses. Unless progress notes document these observations, there is no way to assess the efficacy of treatment.

Examples of clinical observations include:

- "The client appeared depressed as evidenced by slumped posture, crying often, and a blunted affect."
- "The client appeared anxious as evidenced by speaking more rapidly than usual, hyperventilating, sweating, and getting out of the chair four times."
- "The child continues to demonstrate defiant behaviors as evidenced by yelling at her mother three times during the session, telling this therapist to "stuff it," and refusing to answer questions over 50% of the time."

Each of these progress note statements clearly documents observations that validate the diagnosis and treatment plan. Without statements of this nature, a third-party auditor or insurance case manager may not find sufficient evidence to warrant payment for additional services. There have been legal and ethics cases in which treatment is rendered to a client, but the progress notes did not clearly document that a disorder existed or was properly treated. Results have led to loss of licensure, malpractice, or other disciplinary measures. Concise documentation helps solve all of these issues.

What Progress or Setbacks Occurred?

Because nearly all behavioral health insurers rely on a medical model to substantiate treatment, and a significant number of clients utilize such insurance to pay for treatment, it is necessary that this model be used to document a client's impairments and the medical necessity for treatment. In this model, treatment that does not alleviate or reduce impairments is not considered helpful and should be discontinued or modified. Consider a person with a broken leg who visited the doctor at regular intervals for treatment. It would be expected that the patient's medical charts would document the specific services provided and any improvements in the patient's condition. If the broken bone began to deteriorate, we would expect it to be clearly documented to help determine necessary changes in the treatment. Mental health services documentation follows a similar format.

Third-party payors will generally stop reimbursing treatment that does not document alleviation of impairments after a number of sessions or after various interventions have been attempted. Some treatments will not work for some clients; however, it is also possible for a client to progress in leaps and bounds but not qualify for reimbursement because progress was not properly documented.

Clinical setbacks do not necessarily indicate that treatment is of poor quality. Setbacks might occur because additional stressors develop during the course of therapy, treatment strategies are not the best fit for the client, the client-therapist match is not optimum, the client is noncompliant, or for a number of other reasons. Documenting setbacks is important because it raises red flags indicating that changes might be needed. Good documentation explains how clinical setbacks were handled and how subsequent changes affected the client's condition.

Clear documentation of progress and setbacks makes it easier for the clinician to consult with other professionals about the case. Examples of progress note statements of progress and setbacks include:

- "Progress is evidenced by client's initiating discussions in session, displaying a normal affect, and no longer crying during session when discussing losing his job."
- "The client states that she has been more depressed and frustrated in the past three weeks because her family is protesting her attempts to be more assertive."
- "The child's mother states that target behaviors in school (hitting teacher, stealing, and destroying property) have escalated to the point of being suspended from school."

What Signs and Symptoms of the Diagnosis Are Present or No Longer Present?

The medical model requires documenting the presence or absence of diagnostic symptoms and impairments. Just as a diagnosis is validated by the presence of symptoms and impairments, progress is assessed by alleviation of symptoms and impairments. In effect, the initial diagnostic interview identifies symptoms and impairments, and treatment attempts to resolve or alleviate them. Most psychotherapies do not actively or specifically focus on symptoms alone as part of the therapeutic process. Symptoms and impairment reduction is a documentation procedure, not a therapeutic technique.

There is a notable difference between a medical model of therapy and a medical model of documentation. A medical model of documentation can be used for any type of therapy, whether it focuses on symptoms, insight, the relationship, cognitions, behavior, or anything else. No matter what theoretical model is practiced, the client will have subjective feelings of therapeutic progress. For example, if a client who previously experienced an average of three panic attacks per day prior to therapy now reports having one or none per day, symptoms have been reduced. The client does not necessarily care about the type of treatment used; what is important is the decrease in panic attacks. Thus, although the medical model is used to document the effects of therapy, it is not needed to determine the process or method used in treatment.

When clients come to therapy, they have a reason for being there. Generally, something in their lives is not going well. Issues might be related to emotional, social, occupational, or other aspects of their lives. No matter how the client is suffering, the reason for coming to therapy is called the presenting problem. If clients are able to detect that they need services due to subjective levels of symptoms and impairments, they will also know when they are getting better. Effective progress notes document these changes in client symptoms and impairments. For example:

- "The client claims to be symptom-free of binging and purging for the past two months."
- "Since the onset of therapy, the client claims to feel increasingly more irritable most of the time."
- "The client states that she is still depressed most of the time."

How Are Treatment Plan Goals and Objectives Being Met at This Time?

Progress notes regularly evaluate the effectiveness of therapy. Measurable and observable treatment plan objectives provide the best evidence of therapeutic effectiveness. Progress note statements may be evaluative or summative, or they may provide current information about the client's progress. Statements of this nature are helpful in making treatment plan revisions. For example:

- "Four out of five treatment goals have been met to date."
- "Objective 2b, "attend work at least three days per week," is met and being revised to "attend work at least four days per week."
- "Little progress has been made in the past two months of treatment, due to noncompliance."

What Is the Current Medical Necessity for Services?

Most insurers require evidence of medical necessity before reimbursing for mental health services. Thus, progress notes should document the medical necessity of services needed by regularly recording the client's functional impairments caused by the mental illness.

According to the medical model, when a client is no longer functionally impaired, services are no longer necessary. Documentation thus helps the therapist and client to decide when treatment can be terminated. When treatment plan goals, objectives, and discharge criteria are written clearly and understood by both the client and the therapist, vagary about termination decreases.

On the other hand, some therapy is rarely, if ever, considered medically necessary, including personal growth, psychoeducational treatment, treatment for non-Axis I disorders, and other types of therapy in which the client is not impaired by a mental disorder. Although clinicians need not necessarily steer clear from those types of therapy, they may have to prepare patients to be prepared to pay the bill themselves. Unfortunately, some third-party payors forbid their contracted therapists from charging for mental health services that are not medically necessary. Some examples of documenting continued medical necessity include:

- "The client has experienced an average of five panic attacks daily, lasting 20–30 minutes, leading to going home from work early or missing work most days."

- "Since the onset of medication and insight-oriented therapy, the client has been able to get out of bed at least three days per week but remains unable to go to classes."

- "Discussed termination of services due to significant progress in meeting therapeutic goals, which has led to a return to normal functioning socially and occupationally."

What Is Being Done Outside the Session to Increase Effectiveness of Therapy?

Although most psychotherapy occurs at the clinician's office, progress is not measured solely in the context of isolated in-office sessions. Although the clinician can observe progress in session, most indices of progress are statements reported by the client or collaterals about behaviors, affect, and cognitions that occur outside the session. Thus, it is important to document these statements as well. Such documentation may include compliance and progress of homework assignments given in the sessions, behaviors generalized from the sessions, and interventions utilizing collaterals. For example:

- "Client reports initiating three conversations at school party, as rehearsed in the previous session. Reports decreased anxiety resulting from rehearsal."
- "Client's spouse reports enhanced marital satisfaction due to increased positive remarks made since onset of marital therapy."
- "Compliance in homework assignments remains at over 80%."

What Are the Client's Current Impairments and Strengths?

Throughout the course of therapy a client's limitations and strengths will change. Strengths will increase due to compliance with effective therapy. But as the effects of therapy impact the client's family and other environmental systems, certain stressors will also increase. Behavioral changes in one family member are most likely to disrupt the family system in one way or another.

Client strengths should be assessed throughout the therapeutic process and incorporated into treatment even though weaknesses and impairments are the focus of therapy in a medical model. For example, if a person injures his or her right arm, use of the left arm is apt to increase because it is a strength. As the right arm heals, there will be less reliance on the left arm. If only the left or right arm receive attention, the healing process will be hampered, due to over- or under-use. Documenting client strengths and stressors could include statements such as:

- "The client continues utilizing social supports, such as family and friends, when feeling an urge to consume alcohol."

- "The client is improving in reducing levels of anxiety by utilizing relaxation techniques employed in therapy."
- "Although the client is learning new coping mechanisms, his family is refusing to trust him to be alone by himself. Much frustration is reported."

OTHER ITEMS PROGRESS NOTES SHOULD ADDRESS

In addition to the items discussed previously, progress notes should include other important information, such as:

1. *Type of sessions being conducted (e.g., individual, family, group).* Progress notes should list specific types of therapy and therapeutic techniques and describe their effectiveness. Some auditors validate the type of therapy via progress notes. For example, if a therapist bills an insurance company for individual psychotherapy but progress notes document that the client is receiving marital counseling, reimbursement may be denied. (Few insurance companies pay for marital counseling.) Billing marital counseling as individual or family counseling is considered insurance fraud.

2. *Goals and objectives addressed in the session.* Third-party payors provide guidelines such as, "Progress notes must reflect the objectives of the treatment plan." Some progress note forms allow space to list the treatment plan objectives being addressed in the session. Even if the form does not have space for this, clinicians should consider listing session objectives to keep sessions on target.

3. *Time-frame of the session: date, starting time, ending time, duration.* Each progress note should list the time frame of the session. This author recalls an audit in which the evaluator complained that noting the length of a session as "1 hour" was not sufficient, stating, "How do I know the session lasted one hour unless you write down both the starting and ending times?"

4. *Signature and credentials of the therapist (initials only are insufficient).* After the session, the therapist should sign the progress note with his or her full signature, including

professional credentials (degree and licensure), which de-
notes professional responsibility for the session. Initials
are not sufficient for such an endorsement just as a check
cannot be cashed without a valid signature.

Poorly Written Progress Notes versus Well-Written Progress Notes

Figure 7.1 illustrates the difference between a poorly documented
progress note and a properly documented one. The following dialogue between a client and his therapist provides background for
the documentation:

C: I'm so upset about everything that has been happening to me.
T: Tell me what you mean.
C: Ever since I was fired from my job everyone is out to get me.
T: Everyone?
C: Yes. My ex-boss at work won't pay for unemployment compensa-
tion. My wife thinks I'm a bum. The police are following me.
My food tastes funny, if you know what I mean. My children
don't want to play with me. Yes, everyone is out to get me.
T: How long have you believed that people are out to get you?
C: Well, I've never trusted anyone completely, (speaking more
rapidly) but I knew for sure a few months ago when my boss
warned me that people at work were complaining about my so-
called "attitude," as she puts it. I told her what I thought about
the situation, and they fired me. (In a much louder voice) I
knew it would happen.
T: What about the police following you?
C: Oh, yes. Yesterday I noticed police driving by the house at least
four times (carefully looks out the window). They were acting
like they weren't looking for me, but I know their tactics. I'm
sure they're bugging my phone. Have they talked to you about
me?
T: And the food tasting funny?
C: My wife does all of the cooking. There's something different in
the taste the past few months. I'm sure she's in on it, too.
Who knows who she's sleeping with now.
T: Now?
C: Yes, we've been married only one year . . . it's my second marriage . . . I've always wondered why she doesn't answer the

FIGURE 7.1
Progress Note Statements

Poorly Written Progress Note

We talked about issues at home and on the job. Increased fears and marriage problems. Spouse is cheating on him. Not communicating well. Complaining about spouse, job, and police.

The progress note does not depict the medical necessity of services. Although the content might be accurate, it is unclear diagnostically, symptomatically, therapeutically, and does not depict current impairments. Even though significant impairments may exist, the evidence provided is so poor an auditor would most likely state that there is lack of justification to continue services. Statements such as "spouse is cheating on him," may or may not be accurate, therefore should be written as a belief, quote, or not at all. None of the questions listed on pages 130–131 were addressed.

Properly Documented Progress Note

Client appeared nervous, tense, and guarded, noting several current stressors. Was easily upset and agitated when discussing ongoing issues. Recently fired from job. Much blaming of others (ex-employer, spouse, police) of following him, spying on him, being unfaithful to him or trying to harm him. Often got up and looked out of the window for police. Confirms having a longstanding history of not trusting others.

Although progress note remarks are brief, they more clearly indicate current impairments, validate diagnostic criteria, and demonstrate the need for further services. The progress note briefly discussed a possible antecedent, (recently fired from his job), resulting exacerbation of nontrusting behaviors (increased paranoia with ex-employer, spouse and police), and impairments (distrust, checking behaviors, affective concerns).

---

phone when I call her in the afternoon. Come on, let's get real (sarcastically). We all can add two plus two. I won't get near her or any of my so-called "friends." Just leave me alone.

SCIENTIFIC MODEL

According to the scientific model, measurements are based on a baseline behavior, and subsequent measures determine a client's degree of change. Without a baseline measure, the level of change is difficult to assess. Baselines may be established in the diagnostic interview and throughout therapy, and progress note documentation can incorporate changes to the baselines. Two documentation methods utilizing the scientific model are commonly used.

Narrative

In this case, the clinician documents various baseline measures that depict current impairments. These measures may be documented in the intake notes, psychological report, treatment plan, or in progress notes. A progress note might report, "Since the onset of Ritalin (15 mg. × 2) the client's teacher reports the client being on task 80% of the time, compared to 50% prior to treatment."

Behavioral Charts

With this method, either the therapist, client, or collaterals chart progress throughout therapy. Progress notes generally refer to the charts to register progress or setbacks. An excellent use of charting to document therapeutic progress incorporates treatment plan goals and objectives throughout therapy. Figure 7.2 illustrates how one picture is worth a thousand words.

PROGRESS NOTE FORMATS

Clinicians use several formats or means of organizing progress notes. The most popular formats are SOAP and DAP. SOAP (Subjective, Objective, Assessment, Plan) progress notes contain four sections, whereas DAP (Data, Assessment, Plan) progress notes include three categories.

Soap	Dap
Subjective	**D**ata
Objective	**A**ssessment
Assessment	**P**lan
Plan	

FIGURE 7.2
Charting Client Progress over Course of Therapy

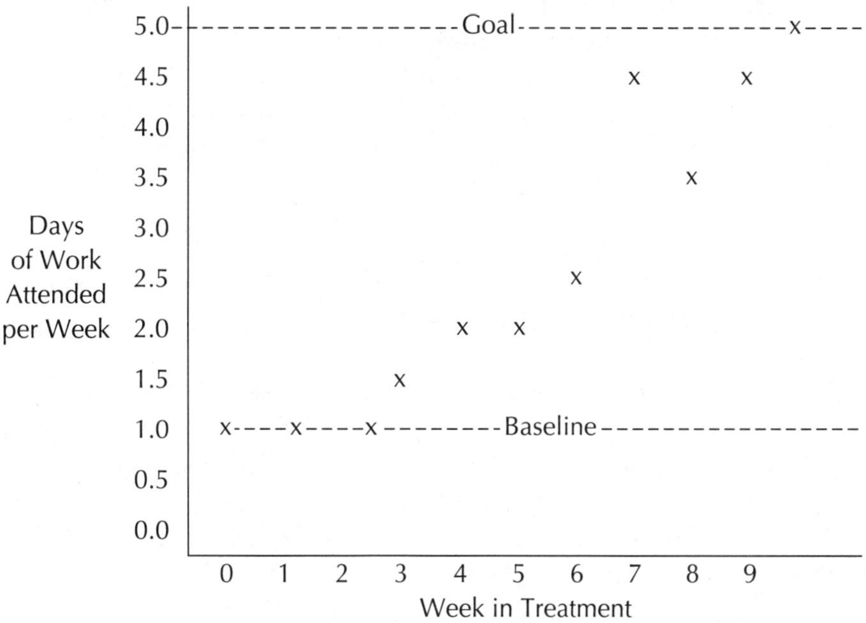

The Assessment and Plan portions of both DAP and SOAP notes are identical. The only difference between SOAP and DAP progress notes is how session content is organized. A DAP progress note lists session content as Data, whereas SOAP progress notes break down session content data into two types: Subjective and Objective.

Data

SOAP Progress Notes The subjective data of SOAP notes are not quantifiable or measurable; rather, they include subjective statements reflecting the client's condition. Information includes the client's presenting problems and historical data (e.g., family background, medical history, and social structure). Examples of subjective data include:

- "The client reports feeling sad most of the time."
- "He states that he is from a dysfunctional family."
- "Several physical concerns were reported such as . . ."

The objective section of SOAP notes represents observable data. Objective data provide specific information that can be compared to previous data or used as a baseline for future objective observations. Examples of objective data include:

- "Current score on the Beck Depression Inventory was 13, which is significantly lower than 28, recorded two months ago."
- "She appeared dysphoric the entire session."
- "On three occasions he cried, stating that he wants to give up trying."

DAP Progress Notes   The DAP format is becoming more popular and is considered by many to be more user friendly than the SOAP format. For this reason, this book will utilize the DAP format. For DAP progress notes, the therapist does not have to separate two types of data (subjective and objective) into different portions of the progress note. Also, some statements, such as "The patient appeared confused, as evidenced by rambling 50% of the session," contain both subjective and objective information that is difficult to separate in the progress notes.

Assessment

The assessment section of the progress note (the same for SOAP and DAP formats) is a written evaluation of the current session and how it relates to the cumulative scope of therapy. Types of information documented in this section are:

1. Effects of the current session.
2. Therapeutic progression.
3. Client's level of cooperation/insight/motivation.
4. Client progress and setbacks.
5. Areas requiring more clinical work.
6. Effectiveness of treatment strategies.
7. Completion of treatment plan objectives.
8. Changes needed to keep therapy on target.
9. Need for diagnostic revisions.

Although it is not necessary to address each area in every progress note, each should be covered sufficiently over the course of therapy. The statements in the Assessment section are summaries of the information in the Data section. Consider each item individually:

1. *Effects of the Current Session* Comments assessing the effectiveness of the session are limited to data collected during the session. These comments are not meant to assess the cumulative effects of the course of treatment. For example:

> "The session seemed helpful in eliciting the client's feelings about how he resents his family intruding on his marriage."

> "The session was not helpful in building rapport."

2. *Therapeutic Progress* Statements assessing the course of therapy document the overall effects of therapeutic interventions rather than the effects of the current session. Third-party reviewers regularly request this information. When progress notes habitually document the course of therapy, the clinician does not have to search for this information because it will be located in the assessment portion of each progress note. For example:

> "The client continues to show steady progress in therapy."

> "Group therapy has not been beneficial to this point."

3. *Client's Level of Cooperation/Insight/Motivation* Client variables require the clinician's careful attention. The best therapy is ineffective without mutual cooperation. The client's level of motivation and insight should be assessed to help evaluate whether the current regimen of treatment is sufficient. For example:

> "The client appears to have adequate insight into the nature of his therapeutic issues."

> "Level of cooperation has increased in the past month, leading to increased compliance in homework assignments and behavioral changes."

4. *Client Progress and Setbacks* It is crucial to document both progress and setbacks. Such documentation provides regular assessments of what positive and negative outcomes have occurred since the onset of treatment. If only progresses are documented, it appears that there is no need for continued services. If only setbacks are documented, it appears that therapy is not helping.

"The client has increased suicidal threats, posing an increased risk to himself."

"Significant client progress is noted in reducing anxiety and worrying."

5. *Areas Requiring More Clinical Work* Throughout therapy, clients will experience changes and stressors. New issues will surface, and others will be alleviated. As the client progresses through therapy, new stressors will develop due to behavioral and environmental changes resulting from therapy. For example, if a client is taught to be more assertive, it may impact the dynamics of the client's family, thereby raising new therapeutic issues. Certain issues that may have been considered minor in the original assessment may develop into significant problem areas. Impairments apparent at the time of the initial assessment might have only a marginal impact upon the client's current functioning level. Current documentation of medical necessity is based on client impairments; therefore, impairments should be assessed periodically to help determine the current need for services. The original treatment plan may suffice for a certain period of time, but eventually the clinical direction will need to be revised. The assessment section allows clinicians to note changes in the client's life that may require revising the treatment plan. For example:

"Slight progress has taken place in alleviating temper tantrums, but school reports indicate continued need to concentrate on this area in treatment."

"The client's excessive drinking of alcohol and not looking for a job continue to cause severe financial and family problems that attribute to client's anxiety and depression."

"The client no longer reports having panic attacks prior to meeting new people."

6. *Effectiveness of Treatment Strategies* Treatment strategies should also be assessed periodically. Strategies that are particularly effective or ineffective should be noted and, if necessary, revised. Documenting whether or not treatment strategies work benefits future treatment providers who work with the client. For example:

"Most progress has occurred when the client is given a homework assignment that corresponds to the session topic."

"Client seems to lack insight, but behavioral strategies are effective in meeting treatment plan goals."

7. *Completion of Treatment Plan Objectives* Third-party payors require periodic updates to the treatment plan. The underlying question focuses on whether the goals and objectives are being met. If they are not being met, or if progress is slower than expected, services may not be considered cost effective. Thus, other services may be more efficacious for the client and should be considered. For example:

"Treatment plan objectives 2, 3, and 4 have been accomplished."

"Client has not been able to return to college by the target date, due to excessive social anxiety."

8. *Changes Needed to Keep Therapy on Target* Therapy is a dynamic process. Problem areas and objectives change on a regular basis. Every setback and achievement sets new directions, no matter how slight. Assessment of needed changes provides a periodic look at the direction therapy is heading and what overall changes will most benefit the client. For example:

"The client is under significant stress at this time, and monthly psychotherapy is not sufficient to meet her therapeutic needs."

"The client seems to be uncomfortable disclosing personal information to a male therapist. This therapist suggests referral to a female therapist."

9. *Need for Diagnostic Revisions* As more information is gathered about the client and life stressors change, the clinician may revise a diagnosis based on more recent information. Some disorders go into remission, whereas others no longer fit *DSM-IV* timeframes. The specific reasons for changing a diagnosis should be listed in the Data (DAP format) section, but the overall assessment of the client should be listed in the Assessment section. Some clinicians periodically assess the current diagnosis by validating current symptoms and restating the diagnosis in the Assessment section. For example:

"Based on additional information, the diagnosis of Oppositional Defiant Disorder will be revised to Conduct Disorder."

"The client continues meeting criteria for Bipolar II Disorder."

Plan

The Plan section of progress notes is also identical for SOAP and DAP formats. Just as the Assessment is based on the Data (subjective and objective types for SOAP notes), the Plan is based on the Assessment. The Plan section of the progress notes documents the focus of future treatment based on the client's current functioning level. Noting future plans for therapy also helps the therapist keep track of treatment options and follow up on assignments. It includes plans for use inside and outside of the session, such as:

1. Homework assignments.
2. Upcoming interventions.
3. Content of future sessions.
4. Treatment plan revisions.
5. Referrals.

Homework Assignments   Homework assignments include any assigned tasks to be completed outside of the counseling session. They range from behavioral assignments, to charting progress, to reading. Homework should relate to the treatment plan and be designed to increase functioning. When homework is assigned, it is important to note it so that it can be discussed at the next session. For example:

- "The client will write a letter to his parents describing his thoughts and feelings about how they treat his sister better than him."
- "Continue logging feelings of anger."
- "Loaned client a copy of, *I'm OK, You're OK,* to discuss next week."

Upcoming Interventions   There are times when a therapist decides to try a new treatment strategy in a future session for reasons such as lack of progress or sufficient progress leading to more advanced techniques. Unless the therapist makes a note, the idea may be forgotten by the next session. In addition, short-term therapy models are often described as "planned and focused." When planning future session topics or interventions, it is helpful to discuss them in advance with the client. For example:

- "Next session: incorporate role playing of assertiveness with best friend."
- "Practice systematic desensitization during the next several sessions."

Content of Future Sessions   Treatment plans generally list at least two or three problem areas that will be addressed during the course of therapy. It is possible to dwell on one problem area for the duration of treatment and never address other areas of the treatment plan. To avoid this, it is helpful to plan in advance when some or all of the client's problems will be discussed and then periodically review the treatment plan with the client to ensure that problem areas are being adequately addressed. For example:

- "Next session: Treatment plan problem area #2, binge eating."
- "Continue treatment of self-esteem issues."

Treatment Plan Revisions   Treatment plans are designed to be revised when client impairments change. This does not mean that the treatment plan must be rewritten each time any progress or setbacks occur. As objectives are met (or not met), they should be revised in an effort to meet treatment goals. New treatment strategies may be added as more information about the client is learned. For example:

- "Current objective: Maximum of five panic attacks daily. Revised objective: Maximum of two panic attacks daily."
- "New objective: Apply for a minimum of three employment positions per week."

Referrals   Any referrals or additional services suggested that affect current treatment should also be documented in the Plan section. For example:

- "Referred to Dr. Smith for medical evaluation."
- "Referred client to Alcoholics Anonymous."

Third-party payors will often ask if a medical or psychiatric referral was given, so it is important to note referrals in the client's chart. The Data section of future progress notes will document the effects of client compliance with the referral. Figure 7.3 provides a DAP progress note for John Doe.

John Doe's progress note follows specific treatment plan objectives and interventions. It validates continued medical necessity by providing examples of current symptoms and impairments concordant with the diagnosis. The treatment is directed toward active symptoms of the diagnosis and it demonstrates therapeutic benefits and setbacks.

Confidentiality Issues and Progress Notes

Some clinicians argue that progress notes should be vague and unrevealing to protect the confidential nature of the session. This argument would be valid if progress notes were meant to disclose confidential material. But well-written progress notes do not need to include potentially damaging confidential information about a client. Some clinicians were trained to produce progress notes that could serve as transcripts of their sessions with clients. These types of progress notes could violate a client's confidentiality if released and are unnecessary. Other types focus on psychological processes rather than the resolution of client problems. These progress notes do validate personal growth but do not demonstrate the alleviation of impairments.

Progress notes can be detailed and thorough without sacrificing the client's integrity or confidentiality. A careful look at progress notes requirements reveals that rarely, if ever, do third parties require clinicians to provide a detailed history of client behaviors (outside the session) in progress notes. Historical information is crucial in the course of therapy, but it is not clearly diagnostic or necessary in documentation. Therefore, there is no merit in recording specific aberrant or private behaviors, thoughts, or concerns that could lead to embarrassment or potential legal jeopardy. VandeCreek and Knapp, cited in Soisson et al. (1987) suggest that records should leave out emotional statements, certain personal problems, information about illegal behavior, sexual practices, or other information that may harm the client or others. None of the procedures outlined in this book are designed to raise confidentiality concerns; rather, they are intended to document the efficacy of therapy.

FIGURE 7.3
Example of Progress Note for John Doe

Progress Notes

Name: John Doe   Date: 7-6-98

Diagnosis: Major Depression, Dysthymia

Treatment Plan Objectives: (1) Identify sources of depression, (2) Describe/understand conflicts with children

DATA: Current Beck Depression Inventory Score: 29. Previous week 27. Did not complete homework assignment due to "low motivation and too many stressors this week." Client reports a very difficult week in which he missed work 50% of the time. Is complying with Prozac (15 mg. × 2), which he began taking two weeks ago. No noticeable benefits or side effects yet. Very dysphoric over feelings of rejection from family. Often cried when relating feelings of worthlessness. Discussed suicidal contract and steps to follow if feeling suicidal. Gave him another copy of emergency contact phone numbers. Interventions included discussing specific antecedents leading to depressive thoughts and cyclical patterns recurring much of his life. Identified three areas that typically lead to depressed mood; (1) perceived rejection, (2) gives up easily leading to guilt, and (3) thoughts of childhood abuse. Role played having a discussion with his children about his depression and his desire to return to previous functioning. Appeared less depressed during the intervention. Client states that on a scale of 100, usual level of depression is at 85, (baseline was 90, last week was 68, objective is 50). Attended a full session of individual psychotherapy.

ASSESSMENT: A very difficult week in which he seems to be regressing into some negative thought patterns that have usually led to depression. Increased occupational and social impairment. Session seemed helpful in increasing insight and increasing hope.

PLAN: Client will attempt to discuss his depression with his children to increase their understanding that he is not upset with them. Continue keeping journal, which we will review next session. Set up med review with Dr. Anderson.

Time Started: 10:00 A.M.   Time Ended: 10:52 A.M.   Duration: 52 minutes

Type: 90844   Next Session: 7-13-98   Time: 10:00 A.M.

                                                                   Date: 7-6-98
_____
Therapist's Signature and Credentials

Other issues arising in progress notes include the client's right to access the information. Although patient records are the property of the provider, the patient controls its dissemination and access to individual records (Soisson et al., 1987). In almost all states, patients have direct access to their records except in rare cases in which the records could be harmful to the patient. When patients inspect records and disagree with their content, they have the right to dispute their content and request needed corrections. Appeal procedures may be incorporated when necessary. Such practices increase the clinician's awareness of, and responsibility for, keeping accurate records, which increases accountability in conducting therapy.

Common Problems with Progress Notes

Vagueness   The most common problem with progress notes is vagueness. Progress note statements such as, "discussed emotions," "went over problems," and "practiced communicating," are common but reveal little clinical information and do not document medical necessity of services or treatment progress. Table 7.1 gives some examples how to make such vague statements clinically relevant.

Progress Notes Unrelated to Treatment Plan Goals   Another red flag for auditors is raised when progress notes do not address the client's diagnosed problem, describe the medical necessity for treatment, or discuss treatment implications. Figure 7.4 illustrates two examples of progress notes that provide interesting anecdotal information but lack evidence of medical necessity. In addition, the notes raise concerns about potential confidentiality violations and provide little information regarding treatment implications.

The Noncooperative Client   It is difficult to adequately document impairments, progress, and compliance when the client is unwilling to disclose information. This dilemma makes it more difficult to demonstrate the medical necessity for services. For example, a client with paranoia is unlikely to disclose debilitating thoughts and behaviors to a therapist (due to the paranoia). In addition, court-referred clients who deny problems with domestic violence, chemical dependency, perpetrator issues, or other criminal areas for which they are in treatment, will often discuss little about their

TABLE 7.1
Making Progress Notes Clinically Relevant

Vague Progress Note	Information Needed	Clinically Relevant Progress Note
"discussed emotions"	Include affective symptoms and qualifiers such as onset, frequency, and duration.	"Client stated feeling anxious this week due to an upcoming evaluation at work, as evidenced by excessive worrying, restlessness, and difficulties concentrating. Reported experiencing a 30-minute panic attack that resulted in a trip to the emergency room. Has had three panic attacks this month at work."
"went over problems"	Define the problem areas in terms of functional impairments.	"Client states being under much stress at work, which is leading to significant decreases in work production. Left work early 3 times in past month due to difficulties coping with coworkers. Believes he is causing others to get behind at work because they must wait for him. Worrying about losing his job.
"practiced communicating"	Identify the treatment strategies involved. Document the effectiveness of treatment strategies.	Role played discussing feelings of anger with a coworker. Reversed roles. Client stated that it is helpful attempting to view the situation from other viewpoints."

behavior. Or they might claim to have a rapid cure in an effort to terminate therapy.

Although insurance companies will initially reimburse treatment based on a diagnosis, they will only continue paying based on the effectiveness of treatment. Thus, for noncooperative clients for whom it is difficult to properly document the course of treatment, you might:

1. Inform the client that third-party reimbursement depends on accurate diagnosis, client cooperation, therapeutic progress, and documented decreases in impairment. Thus cooperating in this process is crucial unless the client desires to pay cash for services. Further inform the client that even if he or she decides to

FIGURE 7.4
Poorly Documented Progress Note Statements

Example A

Poor example of progress note statement

"Client's deceased uncle, Jay Doe, sexually molested him twenty years ago."

Problems with this statement

1. Does not document how this event affects the client at this time (lacks medical necessity).
2. Implicates the uncle (by name) because it is written as a definitive statement. It is possible that the incident did not take place. In such cases, it is better to quote patient directly. Otherwise, if the client, another relative, or the court were to gain access to the client's file, this potentially unmerited and libelous accusation could be used against the client.

Clinically relevant progress note statement

"Client reports a traumatic incident twenty years ago at age 15, in which he states a deceased relative 'sexually molested' him, currently resulting in recurring nightmares, social withdrawal, and fear of older men."

Why this statement is relevant

The historical incident is alluded to; however, the current symptoms and impairments resulting from the alleged incident are the focus of the progress note. For some, experiencing a severe stressor will not cause a mental health problem; in this case, the effects of stress did cause mental health issues.

Example B

Poorly written progress note statement

"We discussed various problems."

Problems with this statement

1. The statement is vague; thus, there is no way of knowing how this fits the goals and objectives written in the treatment plan.
2. There is no reference to therapeutic techniques or interventions employed in treating the client's problems.

FIGURE 7.4 (Continued)

Clinically relevant progress note statement

"Due to increasing social withdrawal and avoidance at work and other areas, we role-played two ways to socially interact with co-workers. Client appeared tense and said, 'What do I have to offer?' Client appeared more confident after role-playing work situations. He stated that he will attempt these strategies by next session and report level of progress."

Why this statement is relevant

This example provides detail without potentially breaking confidentiality if an outside source had access to the record. It documents that social and occupational impairments are currently taking place and validates dysphoric observations. The effects of treatment strategies were noted, evaluated, and incorporated into the client's life.

Note: When the law requires reporting an incident such as child abuse, intended suicide, intent to harm someone, or taking illegal drugs during pregnancy, it is suggested that the clinician quote what the client stated in the session. The client must be warned of limits to confidentiality prior to receiving services.

pay cash, the referral source (i.e., a judge or probation officer) may require evidence of progress as part of the rehabilitation process. If the client still refuses to cooperate, other forms of rehabilitation (incarceration, day treatment, and so forth) may be required.

2. Increase the use of collaterals in therapy when the client may be attempting to cooperate but has poor insight. Collaterals may be useful in documenting behavioral changes outside of the counseling sessions. The use of charts and behavioral change graphs provide evidence of progress. For example: "Client's spouse states that he previously consumed at least two quarts of vodka per day. Since the onset of treatment and med. management, he has remained dry. There have been two incidents of temper outbursts (verbal) in the past month. She states that prior to treatment, temper outbursts (physical and verbal) occurred almost daily."

Therapists should be careful about accepting third-party payment for clients who do not want to be in therapy. Poor rates of compliance impede adequate documentation of progress, and it is challenging to elicit information about the client's ongoing impairments. If such cases are audited, there is a good chance payback will be required. Thus, the clinic will suffer financial losses from seeing such clients. Worse yet, some third parties contractually prohibit clinics from billing the client for penalties issued due to an audit. Even when back-billing the client is allowed, the chances of collection are low, considering the therapy may have been conducted a few years prior to the audit. Finally, it is always more difficult to collect payment from clients who did not want to be in therapy in the first place.

SAVING TIME IN WRITING PROGRESS NOTES

Approximately 75% of more than 2,000 therapists surveyed by this author say they write their progress notes after the session. These therapists note that they prefer waiting until after the session ends because:

1. "I can't attend to my client if I'm writing notes."
2. "Clients will hold back information or become self-conscious if they believe that I am writing everything down that they say."
3. "They will ask me what I am writing down, become interrupted, and won't concentrate on the session."
4. "I wait until I'm finished with the session so I can integrate the whole picture of what was said."

Others write brief notations during the session and integrate them after the session. Few therapists write the bulk of their progress notes during the session. Although there is nothing wrong with any of these procedures, writing progress notes during the session is a time-saver. Imagine a clinician who sees six to eight clients during the day and saves writing progress notes for all clients until the end of the day. The clinician may get a week or two behind and realize there are 30 or more progress notes to write. Now the clinician requires a full day to catch up. Additionally, remembering specifically what took place in each session becomes a mammoth task.

To avoid having to remember specific details about a session weeks later and to avoid falling behind, writing progress notes during the session can be a life saver. Although the previously mentioned concerns about writing progress notes during the session can occur, with practice in session note-taking can be used positively and can enhance empathy. When the clinician nonverbally expresses that what the client says is important by writing things down, clients will often encourage this practice. The time it takes to write a progress note takes only a small fraction of the session time because only the Data section is completed. The Assessment and Plan sections will be completed when the client leaves. For example, in Figure 7.3, the Data section consisted of less than 15 sentences. Thus, for the session time in Figure 7.3, fewer than one sentence would need to be recorded every 3½ minutes.

Data are specific pieces of information that do not require continuity or interrelationships, thus it is not necessary for the Data section to read like a summary. The data are integrated and used to formulate the Assessment section of the progress note after the session. The Assessment and Plan sections can be written as the client leaves the room. The average time to write these sections is generally less than 5 minutes. If a session lasts 45 minutes, and it takes 5 minutes to write the Assessment and Plan sections, it leaves the clinician 10 minutes for a breather before seeing the next client.

Another advantage of writing progress notes during the session is that the therapist can more easily quote clients directly and document observations. Much of this information becomes lost if writing data is deferred for several minutes, hours, or days.

You're well on your way to ensuring that you'll never be held responsible for third-party paybacks. Unfortunately, sometimes even the best planned treatment does not fully alleviate a client's symptoms or impairments in the allotted time frame. In such cases, clinicians must request additional treatment for the client. Convincing third parties that additional therapy is medically necessary is challenging but can be accomplished if the right procedures are followed.

HIGHLIGHTS
of Chapter 7

★ Accurate progress notes are crucial because they are the only evidence of progress, therapeutic procedures, and current mental condition.

★ Although progress notes are detailed, they do not need to reveal information that might potentially harm the client or others.

★ Vague or incomplete progress notes could lead to legal, ethical, or reimbursement issues.

★ Well-written progress notes enable a new therapist to quickly resume therapeutic services during times of therapist transition.

★ Progress notes reflect the client's progress in specific treatment plan objectives.

★ Standard progress note formats, such as SOAP and DAP, follow the scientific method in which the effects of treatment are assessed and a plan is made for future interventions.

★ Time can be saved by writing progress notes during the session.

★ Progress notes are not written from a particular theoretical school of thought, but rather, are simply behavioral evidence of the progress from any therapeutic viewpoint.

★ Research indicates that therapists can learn new means of writing progress notes when appropriate feedback is available and procedures are simplified.

8

Documenting the Need for Additional Services

Most insurance and managed care companies require a special request for additional services once a maximum number of services have been utilized. It is not uncommon for a third-party payor to initially authorize 2 to 5 sessions, then require documentation that additional services are medically necessary. The content and quality of this request directly affects the third-party payor's decision to pay for additional services. It is the most crucial piece of documentation material needed to continue services. A sample preauthorization request can be found in Appendix A.

Because the third-party case manager does not have direct contact with the patient, the only information available is the written mental health records. It is possible for a patient to be in dire need of services, but if the therapist doesn't adequately document this need, services could be denied. The third-party payor should not be blamed or held responsible for denying services when documentation does not clearly demonstrate medical necessity.

Information that third-party payors commonly request is not difficult to provide if accurate records have been kept. The therapist does not have to spend much time trying to remember why services are necessary. Written progress notes regularly document medical necessity. There are several types of information typically requested in a preauthorization for additional services request.

- *Primary and secondary diagnoses.* The preauthorization request should include the most current diagnosis. Axis II concerns should be treated secondary to Axis I issues to ensure third-party payment. Any diagnosis changes should be incorporated into the treatment plan and clearly explained. In addition, some third-party payors no longer provide payment for certain diagnoses such as NOS diagnoses, conduct behaviors, adjustment disorders, or other diagnoses with a GAF over 60.

- *Service dates and current number of sessions used.* This type of information should correspond with the dates on the progress notes. Third-party payors will pay special attention to this information as the number of sessions increases by comparing the number of sessions used to national averages of sessions for various diagnoses. If the number of sessions is significantly more than average, it is important to clearly document any special circumstances that demonstrate a need for additional services. There have been cases in which some managed care companies have not renewed providers' contracts because the clinicians consistently used more sessions than the norm.

- *Current mental status and diagnosis documentation.* This information is crucial for obtaining additional services. The key term is *current*. Clinicians must provide an up-to-date validation of the patient's condition. It should reflect progresses and setbacks that have occurred since the onset of treatment. If there is not current documented evidence of a mental health diagnosis, services may be terminated.

- *Current functional impairments.* Since part of the definition of medical necessity includes functional impairments, services should be able to continue when the patient continues being impaired but shows progress since the onset of treatment. Thus, the clinician should document and validate the current impairments rather than listing the client's impairments at the onset of treatment.

- *Therapeutic/behavioral progress and regressions.* Some therapists view reporting progress and setbacks as a Catch-22 situation. That is, if clinicians emphasize current impairments and regressions as the evidence that additional services are needed, it will appear that no progress has occurred and make services appear unhelpful on paper. On the other hand, if clinicians emphasize great leaps and progresses, it will appear that no further services are needed.

Both progresses and setbacks need to be balanced in the request for additional services report. When progress has occurred but setbacks and impairments still exist, which is often the case, clinicians should provide evidence of both. Ideally, the clinician would document client progress as the result of achieving some treatment plan goals and objectives and document setbacks and continued impairments as areas that have not yet been treated in therapy or as new stressors that have emerged. In this scenario, there is evidence that treatment is working, but more services are necessary to deal with issues not yet treated.

The clinician must exercise ethics in this documentation to prevent painting a different picture of the client on paper than what is actually the case. There may a temptation to overdocument in order to obtain more services. A good check and balance is to share reports of progress and setbacks with the client.

- *Patient's willingness to accomplish treatment goals and objectives.* Client cooperation is necessary in the counseling process. The preauthorization request should include specific examples of client cooperation in areas such as attending sessions, homework cooperation, therapeutic compliance, and behavioral changes outside the session.

- *Revised or updated treatment plan.* Treatment plans are made to be revised. Without revisions, it is implied that no progress has taken place. Objectives should be periodically revised as clients more closely reach their goals set in the treatment plan.

- *Objective discharge criteria.* Discharge criteria are difficult to determine. Vague statements suggesting discharge criteria such as, "attain 80% of goals," mean very little clinically. The best descriptions are in behavioral terms, suggesting alleviation of functional impairments that led to the medical necessity of services.

HIGHLIGHTS
of Chapter 8

★ Most third-party payors request written evidence (generically called a preauthorization request) of the effectiveness of treatment in order to reimburse services after a few visits.

★ The therapist's documentation and writing skills can directly impact the chances of the client receiving additional services.

★ The preauthorization request provides an overview of the client's current mental condition compared to the client's condition at the onset of services, thus measuring clinical effectiveness.

★ Both setbacks and progresses of therapy are documented to demonstrate the need for additional services and the benefits of services rendered to date.

★ The preauthorization request should demonstrate that treatment has focused on the diagnosis by means of the treatment plan.

A Appendix

Documented Client Chart for Judy Doe

Appendix A provides additional samples of completed documentation. Some of the formats and procedures are different than those in the text to provide a wider array of examples. For example, the John Doe example throughout the book often emphasizes using specific forms, such as the initial assessment form, in documentation. Documentation can also be narrative as indicated by the examples in this appendix.

DIAGNOSTIC ASSESSMENT REPORT

Name: Judy Doe   DOB: 4-5-75   DOE 7-8-98

PRESENTING PROBLEM

Signs and Symptoms

Judy Doe, a caucasian female, age 23, never married, is self-referred for counseling services due to excessive worrying and nervousness. She states that she feels anxious and usually panics whenever she is in public places where she may not be able to get away immediately.

During the interview she appeared to be quite anxious. She often fidgeted, breathed rapidly, stuttered a few times, and showed poor eye contact. She reported having a panic attack in the waiting room prior to the interview.

She began experiencing panic attacks three months ago, approximately one month after losing her job as a videographer,which she held for three years. She currently experiences up to 5 panic attacks per day, each lasting 20–30 minutes. When she has panic attacks she reports shortness of breath, choking sensations, palpitations, dizziness, chills, and a feeling of doom. Since her first panic attack in public two months ago, she refuses to go to public places, such as malls or grocery stores, stating that it is too anxiety-provoking. At home she experiences fewer panic attacks except when the doorbell or phone rings. She will not go out with her friends or relatives and states that she is afraid to apply for another job, noting that she is a "mess-up" and "no one wants to hire a has-been."

History of Present Illness

Judy Doe reports no known family history of mental health treatment. She has never attended a counseling session, nor has she been previously diagnosed with a mental health condition. Most of her life she has been somewhat withdrawn and anxious in public, viewing herself as "shy." She reports that she began feeling increasingly more anxious at work when a "college graduate" was hired in a position similar to hers. The college graduate was eventually promoted in the company due to exceptional work quality. Judy Doe became fairly upset and admits that her work quality suffered from her increased amount of worrying about her job. She began making a greater number of errors and missing work due to headaches and upset stomach. After another "college graduate" was hired, she states her work quality became "poor." She was eventually fired.

Since leaving her job, her anxiety level has increased. She feels incapacitated in her ability to work competitively with people who are more highly trained than her. She worries excessively that if she were able to go back to work that she would just get fired again. One month ago she filled out three job applications and received a phone call for an interview. On the day of the interview she arrived at the building of the meeting, panicked, and drove home. When she arrived home she claims to have felt relieved of much of the anxiety.

BIOPSYCHOSOCIAL ASSESSMENT

Judy Doe is the youngest of five children and describes her family as close knit. Her parents have been married for 40 years. She reports that she is from a functional family who treated her "too well" as a child. She describes herself as "daddy's girl" and "the baby of the family." Until she began working full time, her parents took care of all expenses. She lived at home, expense-free, until two years ago.

She currently lives alone in an apartment. Her parents and most of her siblings live within five miles of her. She talks with them on the phone regularly. Two of her sisters visit her at least once per week. About once per month she will visit their homes or her parents in the evening, but may experience panic symptoms in transit. She describes her family as "supportive." Her best friend, whom she has known for over 10 years, recently moved to California due to a job transfer. She has no other close friends.

Her primary schooling was noneventful. She was in mainstream classes and earned average grades. She had few friends in high school and graduated five years ago with average grades. She subsequently attended Tech Institute for one year of a two year program and majored in videography. She left the school after being offered a position at her most recent job where she worked until three months ago. Technical school was very difficult for her academically.

As a child she had few friends and was not involved in any school or outside activities. Others often teased her due to her small size and occasional stuttering. Her older siblings often protected her from teasing and ridicule, but she often worried about what would happen if they were not present. She dated a few times as a teenager and early adult but was involved in no serious relationships. She states that she is too "reserved" and "afraid" to phone any of her acquaintances or former work associates to enhance her social life, but she wishes she were able to learn how to make friends.

She has not made any new friends since graduating from technical school. She usually talks with one of her neighbors on weekends. They have a planned trip to Colorado this coming summer. She attends religious services approximately twice per month, which she finds comforting. Her spiritual beliefs and thoughts are very important to her, and she views them as a definite strength. She describes the people at her place of worship as friendly. She has been asked to join a singles group there but hasn't yet made up her mind about joining.

Prior to developing panic symptoms she enjoyed weekly visits to the zoo by herself. At times she would take her two nieces with her. She played on a neighborhood softball team two years ago, but her friend, who urged her to join the team with her, moved away. She did not continue with the team. She still attends family social functions, such as birthday parties, but is not willing to go to events not involving her family. Prior to impairment, she was willing to attend public events if invited by others. She enjoys camping with two of her sisters and their families.

Her last physical evaluation was conducted six months ago by Dr. Anderson, of Main Health Clinic. She states that exam indicated no health concerns. No medications are prescribed. She is allergic to penicillin. Her weight is within normal limits for her height. She was hospitalized once in her life for a tonsillectomy at age nine. She visits the dentist once per year for routine check-ups. She reports no significant physical traumas occurring in her life.

She rarely drinks alcoholic beverages and has never tried illegal drugs. She claims that she has been intoxicated one time in her life, three years ago, when she was camping with her sisters. There is no family history of chemical dependence. She has no history of arrests or incarcerations for any reason.

Although she has never been in counseling, she believes it will be helpful because her friend successfully went through counseling following her divorce. She is looking for a female therapist "who understands what it is like being the youngest in a family."

MENTAL STATUS EXAM

Clinical Observations

She appeared at the interview neatly dressed and groomed. Posture and health seemed to be in the normal range. Nails were very short, as if bitten. She appeared to be her chronological age. There were no unusual mannerisms or gestures. She was alert. Gait was normal. She sat somewhat rigidly and did not appear relaxed. Eye contact increased as the interview progressed.

Speech was clear and easily understood. She provided a normal range of vocabulary, details, and reaction time. Volume was soft. She did not mumble, slur, or stutter. There was nothing unusual about her speech.

She was cooperative, answering every question. She seemed somewhat inhibited socially, as evidenced by not initiating interactions, but rather responding when spoken to. She did not appear to be defensive, guarded, defiant, manipulative, or hostile. She seemed to be interested in the interview process.

Stream of Consciousness

There was no evidence of a thought disorder. No concerns were noticed regarding issues with thought processes, content of thought, thought disturbances, hallucinations, illusions, or depersonalization. She denies any history of suicidal thoughts, preoccupations, delusions, or detachment.

Affect/Mood

Affective observations included a restricted range of affect concordant with her speech and ideas. Mobility and intensity of affect were within normal limits. Predominant mood was neutral. No psychomotor concerns were observed. She appeared to be anxious, as evidenced by fidgeting with her fingers often. She asked to go to the rest room two times during the interview. She did not appear to be irritable or angry.

She states that she is able to show a normal range of affection toward her family, but not "outsiders." She denies having any anger management issues. When upset she usually holds it in rather than expressing it to others. She denies currently feeling depressed, but claims to be frustrated with herself due to being unemployed. She does not endorse symptoms suggesting a depressive disorder, mania, nor PTSD.

She currently endorses symptoms and impairments concordant with Panic Disorder with Agoraphobia. Symptoms include abrupt development of heart palpitations, sweating, shortness of breath, chest pain, a feeling of choking, dizziness, and chills. She reports that she has had four panic attacks, each taking place when she had to be in public. She has not been able to feel comfortable in social settings, noting major impairments in which she is beginning to feel isolated and not able to apply for a new job.

She further states that for most of her life she only gets involved in activities if she is sure that she will be accepted and liked. In social situations she is often preoccupied with thoughts that people will criticize or reject her. On two occasions she stated that she is "not as good as other people" academically, socially, and on the job. She has taking relatively few risks in her life. She meets criteria for Avoidant Personality Disorder.

Sensorium/Cognition

She was in touch with reality, able to hold a normal conversation, and was oriented × 3. Attention and concentration were within normal limits as evidenced by counting to 40 by threes beginning with one and counting backwards by sevens from 100. She repeated six digits forward and four digits backward, which is within the normal range. She correctly spelled words backward. She recalled three out of three words after five minutes and two out of three words after 30 minutes. Short-term, long-term, and immediate memory were intact.

She appeared to have average intelligence. Level of judgment and abstract thinking suggests age-appropriate behavior. She seems to have appropriate insight into the nature of her concerns, stating that she wants to return to work and learn how to cope with current anxiety. She does not meet criteria for a particular personality disorder but has dependent and avoidant features. There was no evidence of a somatoform disorder.

TESTING

MMPI-2

MMPI-2 results appear to be valid. She finished the testing in a normal time span, responding to every question. Validity scales indicate that she sees herself as experiencing a significant number of problems at this time, which is concordant with the presenting problem.

The basic profiles indicate a 7–0 profile with a slightly elevated 2 scale. People with similar profiles tend to have issues with insecurity, social withdrawal, lack of drive, shyness, and a lack of assertiveness and confidence. The most notable elevation in the profile suggests concerns with anxiety, which is often indicated by longstanding patterns of worrying and poor coping mechanisms. Similar profiles also may indicate concerns with passive aggression.

SUMMARY AND DIAGNOSIS

Judy Doe is self-referred for individual counseling due to panic attacks and resulting social impairment. Symptoms began after losing her job four months ago. She further notes symptoms of increased worrying and difficulties going out in public due to panic attacks. She has no counseling history, nor are there any mental health concerns in her family.

She describes her childhood history in positive terms. Being the youngest, her family often took care of most of her needs. Her family is currently supportive. As well, she has one life-long friend who recently moved out-of-state. She describes herself as being in average health.

The MSE indicated a normal appearance, speech, and attitude toward this examiner. There was no evidence of a thought disorder. She was fidgety much of the interview and appeared anxious. MMPI-2 testing was concordant with the presenting problems and MSE observations. Memory and concentration were within normal limits. She endorsed symptoms and impairments indicating Panic Disorder with Agoraphobia and Avoidant Personality Disorder.

AXIS I: 300.21   Panic Disorder with Agoraphobia

AXIS II: 302.81   Avoidant Personality Disorder

AXIS III: Defer to Physician

AXIS IV: Unemployment, few friends

AXIS V: GAF = 62 (current)   79 (highest in past year)

_____   _____

Signature and Credentials of Therapist   Date

PROGRESS NOTES

Client: Judy M. Doe   Date: 7-22-98

Diagnosis: Panic Disorder with Agoraphobia, Avoidant Personality Disorder

Objectives for Session: 1) relaxation techniques 2) med referral 3) anxiety sources

DATA: First therapy session since intake. On time. Signed release of information with Dr. Erikson. Reviewed limits of confidentiality. Reviewed MMPI-2 results, which suggested anxiety, shyness, and concerns with lack of assertiveness. She concurred with results. Client reports a daily average of 5 panic attacks each lasting 20–30 minutes in past week; each time when anticipating going to public places. She states, "I just can't stop them from happening . . . the harder I try, the worse they get . . . I'll never get a job." Insists on keeping therapy sessions in the mid-afternoon when there is little traffic. Practiced muscle relaxation in three major muscle areas and deep breathing exercises. Initially became more tense when trying to relax. Eventually stated that she felt "more relaxed." Looks forward to daily telephone calls from her family, stating that she "needs them." Discussed feelings of dependency and need for approval. She replied, "That's what families are for." Attended a full session of individual psychotherapy. Topics included test results, relaxation, and family dynamics.

ASSESSMENT: Slight increase in number of panic attacks. Somewhat pessimistic about employment at this time. Seemed tense in learning relaxation techniques; eventually soothed. Supportive family but concerns with dependency. Her attempts to curtail panic attacks increase anxiety.

PLAN: Will practice two relaxation techniques daily. Will write diary of feelings after talking with family on telephone. Next session: Continue relaxation training and family dynamics, review diary.

Time Started: 1:30 P.M   Time Ended: 2:15 P.M.   Duration: 45 minutes

Type: 90840   Next Session: 7-29-98   Time: 1:30 P.M.

_____   Date: _____
Therapist's Signature and Credentials

PROGRESS NOTES

Name: Judy M. Doe   Date: 7-29-98

Diagnosis: Panic Disorder with Agoraphobia, Avoidant Personality Disorder

Objectives for Session: 1) relaxation techniques 2) family dynamics

DATA: Session 2. Med evaluation will be this week with Dr. Erikson. Compliant with homework. Has not looked into any job possibilities. Reports four panic attacks this week, in which she tried repeating relaxation techniques. Although these techniques did not stop them, they may have decreased duration of attacks. Stated that she feels helpless during an attack and "always" phones home when in distress. Journaling notations indicate relief of stress when in contact with family. Brought up increasing resentments toward family due to "taking care of me . . . I want to make my own mistakes." Family will be incorporated as future collaterals in treatment. Reviewed and refined two relaxation techniques. Used guided imagery techniques in imagining going to grocery store. Some resistance but followed through. Gave her a handout of assertiveness training group at Main Hospital. Attended full session.

ASSESSMENT: Cooperative and motivated to change but has difficulties acknowledging dependence on family for stress alleviation. Guided imagery techniques were helpful. Deep breathing seems more effective than muscle relaxation at this time. Somewhat reluctant to join group at this time.

PLAN: Assigned readings. Client will discuss collateral sessions with family parents and two sisters. No changes in objectives.

Time Started: 1:30 P.M. Time Ended: 2:15 P.M. Duration: 45 minutes

Type: 90844   Next Session: 8-5-98   Time: 1:30 P.M.

_____ Date: _____
Therapist's Signature and Credentials

REQUEST FOR ADDITIONAL SERVICES

Client's Name: Judy M. Doe   Date: 7-29-98

Primary Diagnosis: 300.21   Panic Disorder with Agoraphobia

Other Diagnosis: 302.81   Avoidant Personality Disorder

Hours used: Diagnostic interview 1½ hours. Individual therapy 2.0 hours

Hours requested: Individual: 10 sessions (4 conjoint with family of origin)

History: No prior mental health treatment, self or family. Describes self as typically shy and nervous prior to onset of panic symptoms. No close friends. Lost job held for three years four months ago. Since losing job experiences panic attacks when leaving the house. Too anxious/fearful to apply for jobs.

Diagnostic Features: Panic symptoms include shortness of breath, choking feeling, palpitations, feelings of doom, dizziness, and chills. Onset: 5–98. Frequency: 3/day. Duration: 20–30 minutes. Severity: moderate. History of avoiding people.

Current Stressors/Impairments: Currently unemployed and under financial stress. Increasing level of panic attacks, anxiety, and worrying causing inability to go on job interviews. No social supports outside of her family, on whom she is dependent. Avoiding most people.

Progress/Setbacks in Therapy: Client reports decreased duration of panic attacks due to relaxation techniques. Gaining insight into family dynamics leading to dependency. Considering assertiveness group. Cooperative, motivated to change. Somewhat reluctant to try new techniques.

Treatment Plan Revisions: No revisions at this point. Presently working on current objectives.

Referrals/Medications: Referred to Dr. Erikson for physical exam and med. evaluation. Appointment on 8–7. No Hx of meds. Signed release of information with Dr. Erikson.

Discharge Plans: 80% of treatment plan goals met. Reduce number and duration of panic attacks to <2 per week lasting less than 10 minutes. Learn relaxation and coping techniques to control anxiety. Regularly search for employment and attend job interviews. Decrease dependency on family. Increase social interactions and assertiveness such as initiating at least one social interaction daily.

Therapist's Signature and Credentials   Date

PROGRESS NOTES

Name: Judy M. Doe   Date: 8-21-98

Diagnosis: Panic Disorder with Agoraphobia, Avoidant Personality Disorder

Objectives for Session: 1) Review of all treatment plan objectives 2) Increase social contacts

DATA: Session 9. Reviewed treatment plan objectives to date. 1) has become proficient in muscle relaxation, 2) Has reduced number and duration of panic attacks—currently averaging 2 panic attacks weekly, duration 10–12 minutes, 3) receiving medications from MD, 4) difficulties following through with implementing new coping mechanisms, 5) has initiated approximately 1 social contact daily, but with people she knew previously. No initial contacts with unknown people. Discussed revisions of objectives. Appeared less anxious than previous sessions. Has attended assertiveness group three weeks in a row; beginning to feel safe. Experiencing some stress when attempting to assert own opinions toward family. Continued exploring family dynamics and social avoidance issues. Has applied for two jobs in past week; did not panic but experienced anxiety. One interview later this week.

ASSESSMENT: Most treatment plan objectives on target for date. Soon ready to work again. Medications effective; no side effects. Continued issues with assertiveness, social avoidance, and withdrawal from strangers that may impact employability.

PLAN: See revised treatment plan. Will schedule approx. 6 more sessions. Homework to introduce 17 self to three new people this week.

Time Started: 1:30 P.M.   Time Ended: 2:15 P.M.

Duration: 45 minutes   Type: 90844

Next Session: 8-28-98   Time: 1:30 P.M.

_____   Date: _____

Therapist's Signature and Credentials

B Appendix

Overview of Outcome Measures

Prior to the late 1970s or early 1980s, mental health services represented only 3% to 4% of the health care dollars spent by employers. But, mental health costs have skyrocketed by as much as 30% to 40% per year, and mental health services grew from 4% to nearly 35% of the money spent on health care by the early 1990s (Lyons, Howard, O'Mahoney, & Lish, 1997). To reduce costs, services were limited and subject to increasing guidelines for approval. Outcome measures have increasingly developed to help determine the most efficient means of providing quality services. The basic questions being asked in outcomes measures are, "What evidence is there that psychotherapy is working?" and, "What types of mental health services work most effectively for whom?" As outcomes measures research has developed, issues have arisen regarding what needs to be measured and how it will be helpful. Table B.1 provides eight principles of outcomes measurement.

Browning and Browning (1996), developers of the Browning Outcomes Survey Scale (BOSS) state that the best judge of therapeutic outcomes is the person who received services; therefore, much of outcomes measurement is based on self-report. The BOSS comes in three versions: intake, discharge, and 6-month follow-up. Both Likert ratings for quantification and comment sections for quality are included for each of several dimensions. The authors suggest sharing the findings regularly with case managers in either a summary format or by providing a copy of the instrument. Copies of the BOSS are available from Duncliff's International at 1-800-410-7766.

Lyons et al. (1997) suggest three dimensions of satisfaction based on the Rand Corporation for the Medical Outcomes Study (Ware & Hays, 1988). These dimensions include technical quality, competence, interpersonal quality, access, and availability and choice of services. Examples of areas to assess are found in Figure B.1.

The material in Figure B.1 is not intended to be a formal outcomes questionnaire; rather, it provides helpful guidelines regarding the type

TABLE B.1
Principles of Outcome Measurement

What to Measure

Principle 1.   Define the goals and objectives of the service and measure their clinical aspects. Do not measure what is irrelevant to these goals and objectives.

Principle 2.   Determine what is important to consumers, providers, and customers of the services, and attempt to include these in the measurement.

Principle 3.   Determine what is possible and practical to measure. Try not to overreach in any single effort. Multiple short-term studies are often more feasible and of greater value than comprehensive but overly complicated long-term efforts.

How to Measure

Principle 4.   Know the existing measurement choices. Do not create a new measure needlessly. Choose measures with relevant databases that provide norms and benchmarks against which to assess consumers.

Principle 5.   Decide who should provide assessments of clinical status based on the nature of the treatment and the characteristics of the consumers served.

Principle 6.   Choose measures that are reliable, valid, brief, and easy to use.

When to Measure

Principle 7.   Always measure at the earliest possible time. Assessment at the initiation of treatment is essential for estimating change.

Principle 8.   Measure again on a fixed schedule, particularly when the end of treatment is not predictable. This method allows statistical options for estimating end-of-treatment clinical status.

From *The Measurement & Management of Clinical Outcomes in Mental Health* (p. 36) by Lyons et al., 1997. New York: John Wiley & Sons. Reprinted by permission.

of information that can aid in an outcomes assessment. The formatting of the questions can range from Yes-No questions, to a Likert scale, to a narrative.

YES-NO QUESTIONS

Statistically Yes-No questions are mainly used as percentages. If the question, "Did your therapist seem to listen to your concerns?" is asked, two types of information can be used. These include specific answers from a particular client and an analysis of how several clients answered this question. For example, outcomes measures from 100 clients might indicate that 72% of clients surveyed agree that their therapists listened to their concerns, and 28% did not agree.

FIGURE B.1
Suggested Dimensions of Client Satisfaction in Outcomes Studies

Examples of Technical Quality Dimensions

Were the educational materials helpful?

Were the medications explained to you?

Did you understand the possible side effects of your prescription when you finished your visit?

Was the equipment in good working condition?

Were the program's policies explained to you?

Was the billing procedure accurate?

Examples of Competence Dimensions

Did you feel your therapist was qualified to provided the care you needed?

Did you find the hospital staff sufficiently well trained?

Did your therapist discuss your treatment plan with you in a manner that you could understand?

Was the intake worker able to provide sufficient information about the available services?

To what degree were you confident that the program staff were skilled in their professions?

Examples of Interpersonal Competence Dimensions

Did you feel that your case manager was concerned with your well-being?

Did you experience your therapist as warm and supportive?

Did you feel comfortable talking to program staff?

Did program staff listen to you when you had a question or concern?

Did you feel that your problems were being taken seriously?

Examples of Access to Care Dimensions

Was the geographical location of your therapist convenient?

How long did you have to wait to see the crisis worker? How did you feel about the wait?

How many days passed between the time you called to request services and when you were able to see your therapist? How did you feel about this amount of time?

How did you feel about the costs of your treatment?

How did you feel about the copayment?

How did you experience the process of obtaining treatment?

Did you have any concerns about the confidentiality of the service? Were these concerns communicated and addressed?

From *The Measurement & Management of Clinical Outcomes in Mental Health* (pp. 50–53) by Lyons et al., 1997. New York: John Wiley & Sons. Reprinted by permission.

The problem with Yes-No questions is that they assume a person totally agrees or totally disagrees. A "No" answer implies that the therapist did not listen at all to the client's concerns, whereas a "Yes" answer implies no problems in this area. When a client fills out a questionnaire with this format (called ipsative), there is no place for partial agreement. That is, if the client believes that the therapist listened some of the time, there is a dilemma as to how to answer the question.

LIKERT SCALE RATINGS

Likert ratings provide answers on a continuum in which a degree of agreement or disagreement with a statement is possible. For example, in the previous outcomes measures question, "Did your therapist seem to listen to your concerns?" the wording would have to be changed to a statement, rather than a question, because a level of agreement is needed. For example, a Likert rating scale could be incorporated for the statement, "The therapist seemed to listen to my concerns." Likert ratings are numerical ratings in which a low numerical rating indicates disagreement and a high rating indicates high agreement. When the highest point on the scale is an odd number, there is a mid-point in which the client is neutral in the response. A Likert scale of 1–7 is commonly used. Some Likert scales use an even number, in which there is no mid or neutral point. An advantage of using an even number is that all scores are to some degree affirmative or negative regarding the statement being rated. Sometimes researchers will combine data to indicate agreement or disagreement (such as in a 1–10 system in which scores of 1–5 express disagreement, and 6–10 express agreement with the statement). Data from Likert ratings, such as those found in Figure B.2, can be used for several possible outcome measures.

Figure B.3 provides an example of Likert rating items.

FIGURE B.2
Use of Likert Ratings in Outcomes Measurement

1. Pretreatment, midtreatment, discharge, and post-treatment scores.
2. Treatment variables (type of, number of sessions).
3. Clinician variables (style, empathy, background, education, experience).
4. Diagnosis (chronic, acute, onset, duration, intensity of symptoms, impairments).
5. Demographic variables (age, race, socioeconomic status, previous treatment).
6. Treatment/medication compliance (attendance, compliance in homework, meds, interventions).

FIGURE B.3
Example of Likert Scale Items in Outcome Measures

Please circle the response which most closely indicates your level of agreement or disagreement with the following statements.

Highly Disagree 1	Moderately Disagree 2	Slightly Disagree 3	Neutral 4	Slightly Agree 5	Moderately Agree 6	Highly Agree 7

"I was given choices about my treatment"

1	2	3	4	5	6	7

"The therapist explained the benefits and risks of therapy to me"

1	2	3	4	5	6	7

"I was treated with respect and dignity by the therapist"

1	2	3	4	5	6	7

"The therapist listened to my concerns"

1	2	3	4	5	6	7

"The treatment plan was clearly explained to me"

1	2	3	4	5	6	7

"Services were performed in a time-efficient manner"

1	2	3	4	5	6	7

"The clinic's policies were clearly explained to me"

1	2	3	4	5	6	7

"The counseling was directed toward helping my problem areas"

1	2	3	4	5	6	7

"I was satisfied with the counseling I received"

1	2	3	4	5	6	7

"The services I received were helpful"

1	2	3	4	5	6	7

"I would return to the therapist for services in the future if needed"

1	2	3	4	5	6	7

USE OF OUTCOME DATA

Ultimately outcome measures most benefit the client by providing the most cost-effective treatment by the most qualified professionals. The process of collecting and utilizing outcomes data helps make this possible.

On an individual level, outcomes data can be useful to the client/consumer, as a motivator that therapy is working and is cost-effective.

The therapist benefits by receiving feedback regarding how well therapy is working and may result in the therapist changing interventions that are not helpful and maintaining interventions that result in progress. Third-party payors benefit in that they are assured that their funds are being used to benefit clients who have paid for such services. When outcome measures indicate lack of progress it provides a flag that current interventions are not alleviating the client's impairments. In general, third party payors request individual outcome measures on a client by client basis. To date, few third-party payors request outcome studies that combine data from several clients. Self-report information is collected on an ongoing basis; therefore, outcomes measurements can be incorporated into the normal course of therapy without imposing cumbersome additional work for the client.

JCAHO has recently mandated outcome measures to organizations they accredit. They are currently compiling a list of companies to analyze data combining information from all a provider's clients, rather than on a case-by-case basis. The data will be used as part of the reaccreditation process. Part of the responsibility of member organizations will be to document how they have implemented outcomes assessment into their practices.

Outcomes measurement in mental health is in its infancy. Most books on this topic have been published in the past 10 years. A few examples include Lyons et al. (1997), Ogles, Lambert, and Masters (1996), Sperry, Brill, Howard, and Grisson (1996), Howard, Orlinski, and Lueger (1994), and Orlinsky and Howard (1986).

Glossary

Abstractive capacity A person's ability to think abstractly. Children often think concretely, whereas an average adult is able to think conceptually rather than perceptually.

Documentation examples:

In the MSE, the clinician often asks the client to interpret various proverbs that could be interpreted either concretely or abstractly. An abstract interpretation of "The early bird catches the worm," could be, "Those who get up early have the best opportunities," whereas a concrete interpretation is generally more literal. A child, an adult with limited intelligence or brain damage might interpret this proverb as, "Birds catch worms in the morning." Tests of abstract thinking may also indicate signs of a thought disorder. Responses such as, "Birds who fly never die if they eat a worm every day to keep the doctor away," generally indicate concerns beyond the normal range of concrete vs. abstract thought patterns.

Activity level A series of observations in the MSE including notations such as a client's mannerisms, gestures, degree of relaxation vs. tenseness, eye contact, vigilance, gait, degree of boredom, attentiveness, and body movements.

Documentation examples:

Increased activity level: "Increased activity level was observed as evidenced by several body movements, tenseness, often getting out of the chair, and hypervigilance."

Decreased activity level: "The client's activity level appeared decreased as evidenced by low attention span, masked facies, psychomotor retardation, and slow speech."

Affective observations The client's degree of affect (emotions) as observed by the clinician. See appropriateness of affect, intensity of affect, mobility of affect, range of affect, and predominant mood.

Documentation examples:

Depressed mood: "The client appeared dysphoric as evidenced by blunted affect, low mobility of affect, restricted range of affect, few facial expressions, and crying at times."

Anxious mood: "The client appeared anxious. Observations included low eye contact, sweating, irritability, and over-worrying."

Appearance Objective observations made by the clinician describing the client's grooming, manner of dress, hygiene, posture, health, demeanor, and apparent age.

Documentation examples:

Appearance suggesting depressed mood: "Client appeared at the interview appearing dysphoric as evidenced by disheveled hair, slumped posture, beard stubble, and lack of facial expression."

Appearance suggesting mania: "The client wore extremely bright clothing not suggestive of his usual appearance. Activity level was increased."

Appearance suggesting thought disorder, dementia, or possible substance abuse: "The client appeared at the interview with a soiled winter coat (in the summertime), mismatched socks, and no shoe laces. There was a strong body odor. He appeared to be in poor health, looking approximately 15 years older than his chronological age."

Appropriateness of affect Affective observations indicating the concordance between the client's stated mood, speech, and ideas.

Documentation examples:

Example 1: "Although the client stated that she was severely depressed and suicidal, she often spoke in an animated manner, joked, and seemed to be somewhat flirtatious."

Example 2: "The client sat in the interview calmly, appearing relaxed, but stated that he was extremely worried and having panic symptoms."

Assessment The continuous process in integrating clinical data to form an objective clinical opinion. Assessment data in mental health comes from sources such as observations, information gathered from others, and standardized testing. Simply reporting data is not an assessment. Generally, the more effectively the data is integrated, the better the assessment. Assessment information is used to determine the most appropriate treatment for the client.

Associated symptoms Symptoms that are often linked to a mental health disorder but not used in validating a diagnosis because they are also prevalent in several disorders.

Examples of associated symptoms: Social withdrawal, difficulties coping, low self-esteem, fatigue, irritability, difficulty concentrating, and several others.

Attention or **attention span** The ability to cognitively focus on a stimulus when in an aroused state. Common MSE tasks to assess attention include incrementally repeating numbers (digit span) forward and backward. Other indices include the examiner's observations of the client's level of attention in holding a conversation.

Documentation examples:

Low attention span: "Client's attention span appeared to be significantly below average, as evidenced by asking to have several questions repeated, repeating 3 digits forward and 2 digits backward, and often staring into space."

Attitude toward examiner The client's general attitude observed during the interview. Descriptions include aspects such as cooperation, level of interest, guardedness, defiance, humor, defensiveness, evasiveness, suspiciousness, manipulative, and level of historical information provided. The validity of the interview is affected by this variable.

Documentation examples:

Negative attitudinal concerns: "Attitudinal concerns were noted during the interview in which the client made several defiant comments, refused to supply background information, made several derogatory comments, and stated that he does not trust anyone with a tie."

Positive attitude: "The client was cooperative, answered every question, provided detailed historical information, and seemed interested throughout the interview."

Axis I: Mental Disorders   A DSM diagnosis describing a mental health diagnosis. All mental health diagnoses in the *DSM-IV* are considered Axis I, except personality disorders and Mental Retardation.

Axis II: Personality Disorders and Mental Retardation   DSM diagnoses of personality disorders and Mental Retardation.

Axis III: Physical Conditions and Disorders   DSM diagnoses of a physical nature. These may or may not have a bearing on mental disorders. Mental health professionals generally defer this diagnosis to a physician or refer to information received from a physician.

Axis IV: Psychosocial and Environmental Problems   A DSM axis which includes a listing of current stressors in the client's life that may be contributing to mental health issues.

Axis V: Global Assessment of Functioning   A overall DSM assessment of the client's current level of functioning on a 100 point scale. It also allows for noting changes in functioning over a period of time.

Biopsychosocial assessment   An ongoing assessment of the client's biological, psychological, and social functioning.

Clinical observations   Any observations made by the therapist regarding client behaviors. Typical observations include aspects such as affect, appearance, activity level, speech, and attitude toward examiner.

Clang associations   A type of loose association in which statements are interrelated by their sounds, rather than meaning.

> *Example:* "I went to Brent at Trent and spent the rent in a dent by a tent."

Cognition   Mental processing of information involving memory and thinking. Mental status observations include indices such as the client's apparent contact with reality, orientation × 3, attention, and concentration.

Collateral information   Background and clinical information about the client provided by other people such as other professionals, family members, and significant others.

Compulsions   Repeated physical or mental acts viewed as not useful to the client. Examples include behaviors such as repeatedly washing hands, locking doors, checking that appliances are turned off, or other excessive behaviors of clinical significance.

Concentration   The ability to focus attention over a period of time. MSE measures of concentration typically include tasks such as counting by serial threes beginning with 1, or counting backwards by sevens from 100.

Documentation examples:

Poor concentration: "Client's concentration seemed to be significantly below average, as evidenced by not being able to count by serial threes beginning with one and sometimes forgetting the topic of a question asked after providing only part of the answer."

Adequate concentration: "The client's level of concentration appeared to be within normal limits as evidenced by rapidly counting backwards from 100 by sevens in a normal time period, making zero errors.

Confidentiality   An agreement between the therapist and client that the information disclosed to the therapist will not be shared with other people without the client's consent. State laws impose certain limits of confidentiality that should be disclosed to the client prior to receiving services.

DAP progress notes   A progress note format in which three distinct sections are outlined including Data, Assessment, and Plan.

Data   Specific information, such as observations, test scores, client statements, and collateral information, that is used to form an assessment.

Delusions   Untrue or incorrect beliefs that are not religiously or culturally approved. Contrary evidence does not change these beliefs. Common types of delusions include paranoid, grandeur, nihilistic, and somatic.

Depersonalization   A subjective experience of feeling detached or outside of one's body or in a dream.

Derailment   A loosening of associations depicted by unrelated thoughts. Clients jump from one thought to another without a logical transition, which is likened to a train jumping off the rail.

Example: A client might say, "I balloon never before Sally pepper chair over there."

Discharge   The time in which the clinician or treatment center no longer holds responsibility for the care of the patient. Generally a discharge summary report accompanies discharge.

Echolalia   Recurring repetitions of another person's speech.

Effectiveness   The level in which clinical interventions and care are provided in accordance to the current level of knowledge and practice in the field.

Efficacy   The level of positive outcomes for the client resulting from treatment.

Efficiency   The correspondence between the resources used in providing treatment and the outcomes of treatment. Sometimes called cost effectiveness or cost/benefits ratio.

Essential symptoms   *DSM-IV* symptoms that must be prevalent for a diagnosis to be made. Also called core symptoms.

Euphoria   An elevated normal mood state. Not a manic state. Often described as a state of happiness.

Euthymia   A normal range of mood states.

Flight of ideas   A rapid succession of interconnected ideas in which the client's conversation changes quickly. The topic of conversation may change from sentence to sentence but logic is retained.

Goals   The client's overall desired outcomes from therapy. The endpoint in therapy.

Hallucinations   Perceptual disturbances without corresponding outside stimulation. Hallucinations are associated with all five of the senses. They are often associated with psychosis.

Illusions   A misperception or distortion of an outside stimulus.

Example: Trees blowing in the wind may be perceived as demons or giants.

Immediate memory   Memories recently stored.

Example: In the MSE the clinician may ask the client to remember three unrelated words after five and thirty minute intervals.

Impairments Areas in a person's life that are not functional; therefore, treatment is "medically necessary." Also called functional impairments. Commonly documented areas of impairment include social, occupational, affective, physical, and academic.

> *Example:* "Due to increased irritability and aggression over the past year, the client currently has no friends or social supports. He has not been involved in any social activities for several months and is becoming increasingly more withdrawn, resulting in social impairment."

Intensity of affect The strength of affective expression that is often put on a continuum from mild to strong.

JCAHO The Joint Commission on Accreditation of Healthcare Organizations is an accrediting agency for health care organizations designed to improve the quality of care from member organizations to the public.

Loose associations The absence or loss of logical connectedness in speech. Speech transitions seem to have little association.

> *Example:* "I like bananas because they taste good and children walk to school."

Malingering The intentional presentation of signs and symptoms of a mental disorder. It is generally intended to achieve some sort of gain or to avoid unpleasant circumstances.

Medical model The medical model views mental health service delivery as treating pathology in which documentation consists of symptoms reduction.

Medical necessity Mental health services are considered medically necessary when significant dysfunction or impairments exist that result from a diagnosable mental disorder.

Mobility of affect The rate in which a person moves from one type of affect to another. For example, if a client moves rapidly from dysphoria to euphoria, it would be described as lability or increased mobility. Little or no mobility is described as constricted or fixed.

Mood The client's description of his or her current or usual affective state.

Mood disorder Mood disorders are classified as diagnoses in mania, depression, or both. Also called affective disorder.

Neologisms   New or nonsense words used by the client but not recognized as unusual words.

> *Example:* "The cirplexanity of the situation leads to additional re-countations."

Objectives   Objectives are sequential steps by which treatment plan goals are met. Each objective, when attained, is revised to more closely reach the goal.

Obsessions   Intrusive and persistent unwanted thoughts that will not go away despite attempts to suppress them and despite knowledge that the thought is not reality-based or is out of proportion to reality.

Orientation   A person's ability to understand his or her connection in relation to aspects such as time, place, and person. In the MSE, the clinician generally states that the person is "oriented times 3" when referring to orientation in all three areas.

Poverty of speech   The client's speech has little depth or meaningful information. Sometimes little is spoken, whereas others may speak full sentences.

Preoccupation   A recurrent theme, thought, or idea often prevalent in the client's conversations or thoughts.

> *Example:* "They're evil. This world is wicked. I dream about the awful things happening. My friends, family, and everyone . . . they're all evil. I always know when the bad people are coming."

Presenting problem   The client's statement of the problem area or reason for seeking services. It is not a diagnosis, but problem areas will be assessed to help determine the need for services.

Prognosis   The clinician's opinion as to the probability of the client leaving services with a positive outcome. Typical descriptions include poor, marginal, guarded, moderate, good, and excellent. It is common for the clinician to also include qualifiers, such as compliance, to the prognosis for areas such as medications, treatment, or changes in areas such as behaviors or education.

Provisional diagnosis   A diagnosis qualifier that is given when there is yet insufficient information to warrant a full diagnosis.

Psychomotor agitation   A behavioral observation in the MSE in which the client appears to have difficulties sitting still, attending to tasks, and/or appears tense.

Psychomotor retardation   A behavioral observation in the MSE in which the client's movements and other behaviors are slow.

Range of affect   The client's ability to express a variety of affective responses in various situations. Descriptors are often depicted as normal, restricted, blunted, or flat.

Recent Memory   Memories of recent events in the client's life. MSE questions, such as the client's memory of recent meals and events of the past weekend, are typically asked.

Remote Memory   Memories of historical events in the client's life. MSE questions, such as the name of the street they grew up on, previous teachers' names, or asking someone born prior to the mid-1950s what they were doing when they heard that President Kennedy was shot.

Signs   Characteristics of a mental disorder are those that are observed objectively by the clinician.

SOAP Notes   A progress note format in which four distinct sections are outlined including Subjective, Objective, Assessment, and Plan.

Somatoform disorder   A variety of physical disorders with emotional origins.

Symptoms   Characteristics of a mental disorder reported by the affected individual.

Thought content   Thought content generally refers to types of thoughts the client experiences. The MSE often includes questions regarding obsessions, compulsions, phobias, suicidality, homocidality, and antisocial thoughts.

Thought disorder   A thought disorder encompasses disorders of thought or perception such as schizophrenia or psychotic disorders.

Thought disturbances   Thought disturbances are thoughts that are intrusive such as delusions (persecutory, grandeur, and somatic) or ideas of reference (thought broadcasting, thought control, or bizarre thoughts).

Thought processes   The manner in which thoughts are interconnected. It is measured in the MSE by aspects of the client's speech such as number of ideas, flight of ideas, relevance, coherence, derailment, neologisms, and associations.

Treatment plan   A systematic plan, formulated by the client and therapist, in which the client's diagnosis, problem areas, goals and objectives, treatment strategies, and anticipated closure dates are delineated. It becomes an agreement, similar to a contract, for the course of therapy.

Bibliography and Suggested Readings

Allen, J. G., Buskirk, J. R., & Sebastian, L. M. (1992). A psychodynamic approach to the master treatment plan. *Bulletin of the Menninger Clinic, 56,* 487–510.

American Psychiatric Association. (1994). *Diagnostic and statistical manual of mental disorders* (4th ed.). Washington, DC: American Psychiatric Association.

Barlow, D. H. (1993). *Clinical handbook of psychological disorder: A step-by-step treatment manual* (2nd ed.). New York: Guilford Press.

Brown, S. L. (1991). *The quality management professional's study guide.* Pasadena, CA: Managed Care Consultants.

Browning, C. H., & Browning, B. J. (1996). *How to partner with managed care.* New York: Wiley.

Cohen, R. J. (1979). *Malpractice: A guide for mental health professionals.* New York: Free Press.

Dalton v. State. 308 N.Y.S. 2d 441 (1970).

Folstein, M. F., Folstein, S. E., & McHugh, P. R. (1975). Mini-mental state: A practical method for grading the cognitive state of patients for the clinician. *Journal of Psychiatric Research, 12,* 189–198.

Frederikson, L. W., Richter, W. T., Jr., Johnoson, R. P., & Solomon, L. J. (1982). Specificity of performance feedback in a professional service delivery setting. *Journal of Organizational Behavior Management, 3,* 41–53.

Fulero, S. M., & Wilbert, J. R. (1988). Record keeping of clinical and counseling psychologists: A survey of practitioners. *Professional Psychology Research and Practice, 19,* 658–660.

Gabbard, G. O. (1990). *Psychodynamic psychiatry in clinical practice.* Washington, DC: American Psychiatric Press.

Galasso, D. (1987). Guidelines for developing multi-disciplinary treatment plans. *Hospitals and Community Psychiatry, 38,* 394–397.

Goldstein, G., & Hersen, M. (1990). *Handbook of psychological assessment* (2nd ed.). New York: Pergamon Press.

Goodman, M., Brown, J., & Dietz, P. (1992). *Managing managed care: A mental health practitioner's guide.* Washington, DC: American Psychiatric Press.

Grant, R. L. (1981). The capacity of the psychiatric record to meet changing needs. In C. Siegel & S. K. Fischer (Eds.), *Psychiatric records in mental health care.* New York: Brunner/Mazel.

Groth-Marnat, G. (1996). *Handbook of psychological assessment* (3rd ed.). New York: Wiley.

Gutheil, T. B., & Appelbaum, P. S. (1982). *The clinical handbook of psychiatry and the law.* New York: McGraw-Hill.

Howard, K. L., Orlinski, & Lueger, R. J. (1994). The design of clinically relevant outcomes research: Some considerations and an example. In M. Aveline & D. Shapiro (Eds.), *Research foundations of psychotherapy services* (pp. 178–195). Sussex, England: Wiley.

Johnson v. United States, 409 F. Supp. 1283 (M.D. FA. 1976).

Joint Commission on Accreditation of Healthcare Organizations. (1994). *Accreditation manual for mental health, chemical dependency, and mental retardation and developmental disabilities services.* Oakbrook Terrace, IL: Joint Commission on Accreditation of Healthcare Organizations.

Joint Commission on Accreditation of Healthcare Organizations. (1997a). *A practical guide to clinical documentation in behavioral health care.* Oakbrook Terrace, IL: Joint Commission on Accreditation of Healthcare Organizations.

Joint Commission on Accreditation of Healthcare Organizations. (1997b). *Comprehensive accreditation manual for behavioral healthcare.* Oakbrook Terrace, IL: Joint Commission on Accreditation of Healthcare Organizations.

Jongsma, A. E., & Peterson, L. M. (1995). *The complete psychotherapy treatment planner.* New York: Wiley.

Jongsma, A. E., Peterson, L. M., & McInnis, W. P. (1996). *The child and adolescent psychotherapy treatment planner.* New York: Wiley.

Kennedy, J. A. (1992). *Fundamentals of psychiatric treatment planning.* Washington, DC: American Psychiatric Press.

Klopfer, W. G. (1960). *The psychological report.* New York: Grune & Stratton.

Lezak, M. D. (1995). *Neurological assessment* (3rd ed.). New York: Oxford University Press.

Lovett, S. B., Bosmajian, C. P., Frederiksen, L. W., & Elder, J. P. (1983). Monitoring professional service delivery: An organizational level intervention. *Behavior Therapy, 14,* 170–177.

Lyons, J. S., Howard, K. I., O'Mahoney, M. T., & Lish, J. D. (1997). *The measurement and management of clinical outcomes in mental health.* New York: Wiley.

Maxmen, J. S., & Ward, N. G. (1995). *Essential psychopathology and its treatment.* New York: Norton.

Medicare program: Prospective payment for Medicare final rule. (1984). *Federal Register, 49,* 234–240.

Morrison, J. R. (1993). *The first interview.* New York: Guilford Press.

Morrison, J. R. (1995). DSM-IV *made easy.* New York: Guilford Press.

Ogles, B. M., Lambert, M. J., & Masters, K. S. (1996). *Assessing outcome in clinical practice.* Boston: Allyn & Bacon.

Orlinsky, D. E., & Howard, K. I. (1986). Process and outcome in psychotherapy. In S. L. Garfield & A. E. Bergin (Eds.), *Handbook of psychotherapy and behavior change* (3rd ed., pp. 217–234). New York: Wiley.

Ormiston, S., Barrett, N., Binder, R., & Molyneux, V. (1989). A partially computerized treatment plan. *Hospital and Community Psychology, 40,* 531–533.

Othmer, E., & Othmer, S. C. (1994). *The clinical interview using* DSM-IV, *Vol. 1: Fundamentals. Vol. 2: The difficult patient.* Washington, DC: American Psychiatric Press.

Patterson, R., Cooke, C., & Liberman, R. (1972). Reinforcing the reinforcers: A method of supplying feedback to nursing personnel. *Behavior Therapy, 3,* 444–446.

Phares, E. J. (1988). *Clinical psychology: Concepts methods, and profession* (3rd ed.). Pacific Grove, CA: Brooks/Cole.

Roth, A. D., & Fonagy, P. (1996). *What works for whom? A critical review of psychotherapy research.* New York: Guilford Press.

Siegel, C., & Fischer, S. K. (1981). *Psychiatric records in mental health care.* New York: Bruner/Mazel.

Slovenko, R. (1979). On the need for record keeping in the practice of psychiatry. *Journal of Psychiatry and Law, 7,* 339–340.

Soisson, E. L., VandeCreek, L., & Knapp, S. (1987). Thorough record keeping: A good defense in a litigious era. *Professional Psychology: Research and Practice, 14,* 498–502.

Soreff, S. M., & McDuffee, M. A. (1993). *Documentation survival handbook: A clinician's guide to charting for better care, certification, reimbursement, and risk management.* Seattle, WA: Hogrefe & Huber.

Sperry, L., Brill, P., Howard, K. I., & Grisson, G. (1996). *Treatment outcomes in psychotherapy and psychiatric interventions.* New York: Brunner/Mazel.

Stout, C. E. (1997). *Psychological assessment in managed care.* New York: Wiley.

Sturm, I. E. (1987). The psychologist in the problem-oriented record (POR). *Professional Psychology: Research and Practice, 18,* 155–158.

Trzepacz, P. T., & Baker, R. W. (1993). *The psychiatric MSE.* New York: Oxford University Press.

Walters, S. (1987). Computerized care plans help nurses achieve quality patient care. *Journal of Nursing Administration, 16,* 33–39.

Ware, J. E., Jr., & Hays, R. P. (1988). Methods for measuring patient satisfaction with specific medical encounters. *Medical Care, 26,* 393–402.

Wiger, D. E. (1997). *The clinical documentation sourcebook: A comprehensive collection of mental health practice forms, handouts, and records.* New York: Wiley.

Wiger, D. E. (1999). *The clinical documentation sourcebook: A comprehensive collection of mental health practice forms, handouts, and records* (2nd ed.). New York: Wiley.

Wiley. (1997). *Therascribe 3.0. The computerized assistant to the psychotherapy treatment planner.* New York: Wiley.

Zuckerman, E. L. (1995). *Clinician's thesaurus: The guidebook for writing psychological reports* (3rd ed.). New York: Guilford Press.

Zuckerman, E. L. (1997). *The paper office: Forms, guidelines, and resources* (2nd ed.). New York: Guilford Press.

Index

Practice Planners™ offer mental health professionals a full array of practice management tools. These
easy-to-use resources include *Treatment Planners*,
which cover all the necessary elements for developing formal treatment plans, including
detailed problem definitions, long-term goals, short-term objectives, therapeutic interventions, and DSM-IV diagnoses; *Homework Planners* featuring behaviorally-based, ready-to-
use assignments which are designed for use between sessions; and *Documentation Sourcebooks*
that provide all the forms and records that therapists need to run their practice.

For more information on the titles listed below, fill out and return this form to: John Wiley &
Sons, Attn: M.Fellin, 605 Third Avenue, New York, NY 10158.

Name _____

Address _____

Address _____

City/State/Zip _____

Telephone _____ Email _____

Please send me more information on:

❑ The Complete Psychotherapy Treatment Planner / 0-471-11738-2 / $39.95
❑ The Child & Adolescent Psychotherapy Treatment Planner / 0-471-15647-7 / $39.95
❑ The Chemical Dependence Treatment Planner / 0-471-23795-7 / $39.95
❑ The Continuum of Care Treatment Planner / 0-471-19568-5 / $39.95
❑ The Couples Therapy Treatment Planner / 0-471-24711-1 / $39.95
❑ The Employee Assistance (EAP) Treatment Planner / 0-471-24709-X / $39.95
❑ The Pastoral Counseling Treatment Planner / 0-471-25416-9 / $39.95
❑ The Older Adult Psychotherapy Treatment Planner / 0-471-29574-4 / $39.95
❑ The Behavioral Medicine Treatment Planner / 0-471-31923-6 / $39.95
❑ The Complete Adult Psychotherapy Treatment Planner 2E / 0-471-31922-4 / $39.95
❑ Brief Therapy Homework Planner / 0-471-24611-5 / $49.95
❑ Brief Couples Therapy Homework Planner / 0-471-29511-6 / $49.95
❑ The Child & Adolescent Homework Planner / 0-471-32366-7 / $49.95
❑ The The Forensic Documentation Sourcebook / 0-471-25459-2 / $75.00
❑ The Chemical Dependence Documentation Sourcebook / 0-471-31285-1 / $49.95
❑ The Couples & Family Documentation Sourcebook / 0-471-25234-4 / $49.95
❑ The Child Clinical Documentation Sourcebook / 0-471-29111-0 / $49.95

**Order the above products through your local bookseller, or by
calling 1-800-225-5945, from 8:30 a.m. to 5:30 p.m., est. You can
also order via our web site: www.wiley.com/practiceplanners**

WILEY